CO:

Introduction 7

PART 1 – Who Are You? 19

Your Values 21

Your Purpose 35

Your Personality 53

PART 2 – What Do You Want? 71

Your Needs 73

Your Decisions 87

Your Feelings 103

PART 3 – Now…What To Do? 121

Create Value 123

The Risk of Not Risking 137

Lean Into Failure 147

Take Responsibility 163

Remain Flexible.. 173

Make Life a 'Get To' 183

Conclusion 193

How to Know What You REALLY Want in Life

Discover who you are, what you want and what to do with your life

JAMES BRANNAN

Copyright © 2021 James Brannan All rights reserved

No part of this book may be reproduced or resold in any manner whatsoever without written permission, except in the case of brief quotations embodied in articles and reviews. These may be used if the book and author are cited.

This book doesn't do the work for you but is here to guide you with thoughts and ideas. The author cannot take responsibility for what decisions and actions the reader takes. The reader must do their work and take responsibility for their choices and actions.

ISBN: 9798755603522

Library of Congress Control Number: 2018675309

DEDICATION

This book is dedicated to my parents: Ian and Joyce Brannan who have always been my rocks!

Introduction

The YOUniverse

Imagine looking up into the clearest night sky. Countless stars drawn together in a magnificent display. Yet all seem to fit together somehow, synchronised in a great gravitational dance.

Now imagine that what you're looking at isn't the stars, but it's inside your brain that you get to see this wonderous show. Brain cells interacting in extraordinarily intricate ways. A miraculous tapestry of energy. Like shooting stars; transmitting in their millions of signals, relaying messages at incredible speeds.

Your perception tells you that you live outside of this, but this is where you really live. It's here, inside your brain, this is where your life happens. This is where you choose how you think about yourself, others and life around you. This is where you form your own invented meanings that shape the recurrent themes and feelings that dominate your life. It's here in your brain that you create yourself; that you nurture, love and support yourself or hurt, damage and destroy yourself. You have your own universe right here inside your brain and it's your choice how you put it to work.

Getting You Here

The human species had to survive to bring you to this existence now. Before your life, generation after generation had to learn the ropes of survival for our species to continue. Your ancestors did what they needed to do, survive and reproduce, with every generation becoming a little more sophisticated than the last. The merger of instinct with knowledge passed down gave each new generation an increasing chance of surviving and living longer.

Survival was the primary drive. After all, if they weren't going to survive, what would have been the point in them worrying about anything else? Be grateful, your ancestors went through a lot to get you here and they achieved it! You come from successful ancestors. They achieved their purpose and now it's time for you to achieve yours.

And so, next time you fail to recognise your true worth, remember your ancestors. Garner in yourself more appreciation for the knowing of what it took to get you here. The creation of you started long before your birth, a lot has gone into your existence. You are worth a great deal indeed. Be humble but believe in your worth. Believe in the value that you can create or offer the world around you, because you're not here by accident.

The Rise of a New Order

We've now reached a stage of human existence where our lives can be about so much more than survival. Compared to the roughness and dangers our ancestors had to face to merely stay alive, you and I now live as if wrapped in cotton wool. Instead of being out on the harsh dessert plains or in a cave with predators nearby, we live in comfortable homes with cushioned chairs and perfect beds. We have established communities with shared values and instead of attacking or robbing each other, for the most part, we look out for each other. For those who don't, we have the law to deal with them. They've laid it out for us, our predecessors. Countless generations suffering the limitations of their time, gradually improving quality of life from hardship and toil. And now here you are in this modern world. And, while you're still a survivor, you're much more than that; you're a creator.

The Modern Dilemma

You still need your survival mechanisms, and they still operate strongly within you. You're not likely to be chased by predators or to have to fight off enemy tribes. However, your survival mechanisms have already saved you from harm countless times. When a speeding car comes round a corner, you need to be quick to jump aside. When standing too close to a high up edge, you need a quick safety response. When an animal threatens, you feel a fear that warns you to draw back. When driving and seeing danger ahead, you need that quick adrenaline response to hit those breaks. When touching a hot kettle or stove, your hand shoots back from it before you know it. In the modern world we still have heights, dangerous animals, aggressive people, landfalls and floods, fires and electric shocks. There are 1001 and more things that could kill or harm you.

We need these survival systems still, but we have a dilemma. If left up to their own devices, our survival systems might do too good a job on our lives. We feel nervous, anxious, worried and stressed at times when we could be taking actions in favour of our wants and needs. Instead of falling prey to a predator, we fall prey to our own fear. At times we might feel hopelessly stuck, staying only with what's familiar to us, even though we feel unfulfilled. We dare not take the risk of doing things that might fulfil us more, for fear of that which is uncertain.

This fear may have served our ancestors well, but it's one that now holds us back from fulfilling our lives. For our ancestors, it kept them from wondering too far from the tribe. After all, that neighbouring tribe may have your skin! They'd likely suspect you were there to steal their food or even try to kill them and take their homes. But life has changed, and so must we if we are to live life fully.

You and I are living in an interesting time. A time where humans are pulled between two powerful instincts. Our instinct to survive and be safe and our instinct of wanting much more than that! As you look around you at the world today, you're caught between a rock and a hard plate. You know you're so much more than a creature of survival and yet the lure of your survival instincts is ever present. This lure doesn't just act upon physical threats either; it floods over into so many areas. We tell ourselves a range of threats:

"Don't talk to that person there, you don't know what they might think of you! Don't go to that new place, you don't know what things will be like. Don't act on that idea, your family will think you've gone mad. Don't do that, if it doesn't work out people will think you're a loser. You'll have no friends…you'll look stupid and be disregarded…she'll reject you…he'll leave you…you'll lose all your money…it'll take you too long." All attempts to keep us with what is familiar to us. Why? To keep us SAFE.

Your survival instincts are only there to serve your survival. They keep you safe, but care nothing for your fulfilment or happiness. You could sit on your backside most of your life, only getting off it when survival needs knock loud enough. You could drink or take drugs or do anything to numb the pain of having a brain that's evolved to do more than merely exist. You could get by and survive a long life, but would you be fulfilled? Our dilemma is that, while without survival fears we might fall prey to real dangers, with them we might fall prey to an unfulfilled life full of fear, frustration and misery.

What's The Answer?

Neither of the above choices are great. We don't want to be run over. We don't want to assume everyone is lovely and fall prey to a gang in a dark alley. We don't want to let our guard down and have someone take advantage of us, ruin our reputation or steal our credit card details. At the same time, we don't want to live a life of stagnancy, do we? I know you want more than that, you wouldn't be reading a book like this if you didn't. If your survival fears are left to their own devices, survive you might, but whether you'll be happy and fulfilled is another thing entirely.

And so, what's the answer? How do we deal with this dilemma? I can only really guide you with one idea and that is the idea of thinking clearly for yourself. Can anyone really offer you the specifics that are right for you? Well yes, but that person is only YOU. You decide what to do with your time and your life. Perhaps the answer is to decide on something that will ensure you can survive, while at the same time you can thrive and really go beyond the anxiety of survival.

About This Book

My purpose in writing this book is to help you gain clarity and understanding about yourself and about what you want in life. I believe that good decisions will always be a by-product of good self-understanding. In this book I will help you reveal to yourself what things are most important to you and how to think about them. You will discover a great deal about yourself through the pages of this book and create a main purpose to point your life towards.

As the saying goes; "your mind is like a parachute; it

works best when it's open". I ask you to open your mind to the information here, let it support you and have great value to you. Read this book actively, engage with it and I promise you; you will gain greater self-awareness and useful understandings of yourself and others. You'll gain greater clarity about what you want, and inspiration focused on what you can do. Together, let's get that magnificent brain of yours attuned to being your best version of yourself. The you that can survive and thrive, create and flourish. Live safely, yet fully and engage with your life and live like the crowning glory of your ancestors; the person you really are.

"All you have to decide is what to do with the time you have been given"

Gandalph, in Lord of the Rings

PART 1
Who Are You?

In part 1 here, we will explore some of the key components that make you who you are. I'm going to guide you to reveal to yourself what your core values are and explain why this can help you in making good decisions. We will also go into some analysis of your personality, allowing you to step back and see your qualities and think about what suits you best. I'm also going to ask you some golden questions which allow you to discover what your life's main purpose might be. I will guide you to create a purpose statement that crystalises this for you.

These three things get right to the heart of you and allow you to see your essence, who you are, what matters to you most and what your life is mainly about. Once you know these, then naturally, you start to gain clarity about what you really want.

With greater self-understanding comes the ability to appreciate yourself. Your self-esteem is going to rise. Beyond this, perhaps the greatest advantage you'll have will be your ability to commit to a course of action, knowing that it's time well spent and it's in your heart to do it. When you are clear on what's most important to you and what you want to achieve in life beyond all else, your life can start to become a smooth, productive flow.

Your Values

"It's not hard to make decisions when you know what your values are"

Roy Disney

The first thing I'm going to guide you to do, in your quest for greater self-awareness, is to discover your values. Subconsciously you already know your values. They operate beneath your awareness and influence your responses, decisions and behaviours. You have already been acting on them and living according to them despite the fact that you may not consciously have known what they are. But it's worth becoming fully aware of them.

What Are Values?

Your values are what you VALUE most in life. They are what's most important to you and they hold significant emotional meaning to you. The reason why it's worth becoming aware of your values is because it makes it easier for you to make good decisions. Decisions that you will be happy with and be able to look back on with no regrets later.

In order to understand your values and align with them, it can be useful to state them in single words. Have a look at the following list:

Freedom

Love

Honesty

Loyalty

Integrity

Commitment

Success

Happiness

Resilience

Generosity

Respect

Honour

Harmony

Dignity

Courage

Determination

Action

Fun

Passion

Adventure

Creativity

Contribution

Certainty

Persistence

Joy

Health

Wealth

Spirituality

Connection

Peace

Acceptance

Tolerance

Security

Safety

Excitement

Decisiveness

Humility

Genuineness

Enthusiasm

Discipline

Appreciation

Compassion

You will have your own priority order of values. In other words, you will VALUE some of your values higher than others. A person's top priority values are often referred to as their 'core values'. These are the ones that influence your behaviours the most. As a guideline, you might think of your top five values as your 'core values'.

How Your Values Affect You

If you decide to support or do something that goes against your core values, there's a good chance that later you'll regret your decision. It might even somewhat erode your self-esteem and play on your mind. But if you stay on track with decisions which compliment your core values, you're more likely to feel good about yourself and have higher self-esteem.

It's also useful to know your core values, so that you can make sense of your reactions to other people's behaviours. When someone does something that seems to go against one of your core values, you're likely to have some negative feelings about it. Likewise, at times, someone might be upset with you, because they interpreted something you said or did as violating one of their core values. If you can talk at the level of values, you might resolve the dispute quickly, without further bad feelings. If you argue based on behaviours, you might not find any resolution. For example, if someone tells you they felt disrespected by you when you said that thing, that's far more useful information than just telling you that you're an idiot!

Dealing With Other People

Understanding the importance of people's values can help us communicate and connect more easily and effectively. Think for a moment about a person whose number one value is Security. How do you think they might respond when you try to persuade them to invest in your new business idea? You might try to convince them by arguing that, though it's risky, the potential is huge! Don't be surprised if they respond with anger as their brain goes directly to defending their value of Security. On the other hand, don't lose heart and think everyone will respond to your idea this way. Imagine you then present your idea to someone who's top values are Adventure, Creativity and Wealth? They might be far more open minded to your idea.

What about a Base Jumping, Surfing, Cliff Hanging, 'Adrenaline Junkie'? Do you think their core values are likely to be Safety and Security? Hmm, probably not. What would you guess they might be? Perhaps: Adventure, Freedom, Fun, Courage and Excitement?

So, are you starting to recognise how your values and their priority, have a major impact on how you think and feel about things? They motivate you towards or away from things. You feel more connected to people who say or do things which appeal to your values and less connected to people who seem otherwise. Fortunately, many values are shared between people. Through medias and in institutions and communities we endeavour to promote the values of Peace, Honesty, Respect and Tolerance. This way we enjoy a more harmonious and safe existence. This grounds us and allows us to pursue other things of value rather than worry all day about our security.

What Are YOUR Values?

Hopefully now you have a good understanding of why knowing your core values will be useful to you. Assuming that's so, I'm going to guide you through a few quick methods to do just that.

Method 1

Go back to the list of values shown and circle the ones that stand out for you. Ask yourself; Which are most important to me? Don't think too long at this stage. Give yourself 3 minutes and do that now.

Method 2

A second way to reveal more of your values is to think of someone you really like and admire and answer this question:

What is it about that person that you admire?

PROMPT:

Maybe it's that they are GENUINE or it's their sense of KINDNESS or COMPASSION. Maybe it's that they have PASSION or MASTERY of some skill. Maybe it's INSPIRATION they give you by their PERSISTENCE. There we go; more values to make note of. Answering this question will help you draw out more of your values. As you think of them, write them in a new list.

Now, let's consider the opposite. Think of behaviours you dislike in others. Perhaps behaviours like stealing, violence or other destructive actions.

What is it that you feel strongly against?

PROMPT:

What gets you feeling angry or upset the most? Is it when someone is DISRESPECTFUL? DISHONEST? AGGRESSIVE? If so, this may suggest you hold close to your heart the values of RESPECT, HONESTY and PEACE.

Keep adding to your list.

Method 3

Think, what else gets you going…. emotionally I mean. What gets you feeling anything strongly? Personally, I get strong feelings when I see a person 'go all out' and perform at the best of their present abilities. When a person pushes themselves, I feel a sense of that person's DETERMINATION. Sometimes it's their COURAGE in the face of uncertainty or their CONVICTION or COMMITMENT. What is it for you? What makes you feel the strongest feelings; good or bad? When these come to your mind, add them to your list.

Finally, Prioritise and Find Your Core Values

Now, look at your list and pull out the 10 values that you feel have the most importance for you above all others. Write them down in a new list and then prioritise them by repeating a simple process of comparing one against another. Allow me to show you. Let's say I have a list of values as follows:

Honesty

Love

Freedom

Respect

Courage

Determination

Integrity

Contribution

Mastery

Peace

I will take the first in the list, Honesty, and start weighing it up against the others, one by one, moving down the list.

Honesty vs Love?

My instinct tells me 'Love' is higher for me than honesty.

So, I now pick 'love' out and go…

Love or Freedom?

Let's say Freedom wins that comparison

I now know Freedom trumps honesty and love and I continue weighing it up against the others…

Freedom or Respect? ….Freedom still

Freedom or Courage?....Freedom

Freedom or Determination?....Freedom

Freedom or Integrity?....Freedom

Freedom or Contribution….Still Freedom

Mastery, Peace?....Still Freedom is even more important to me.

Ok so I put Freedom at the top of the pile. Freedom is my number 1 value above all others. Start a new list next door and put Freedom at the top.

Now go again with the next one down; 'Honesty'. Compare it with all moving down the list except Freedom which I can now cross off that list. Keep going until you have your top 10 values in priority order.

Once done…especially take note of your top 5 values. These are your 'Core Values' and I suggest you write them out and keep them close by so you can review them regularly.

Summary

From working with this chapter, my hope is that you feel clearer now about one of the key factors behind human behaviour. You have a deeper insight into what so often creates conflict between people and how you could resolve it. You now know your core values and you can make decisions based around these. If you are ever unsure of whether to do something or not, ask yourself if doing it is being true to your core values. If so, then do it, you'll be glad you did. Be willing to review your value list and make changes now and then if they feel right. Perhaps the greatest benefit of knowing your values, is knowing yourself better. Understanding more about who you are and what you stand for in life brings with it self-assurance and confidence. Knowing your values helps you to find greater purpose in life and that is what we will come to next.

"Peace of mind comes when your life is in harmony with true principles and values"

Steven Covey

Your Purpose

"The two most important days of your life are the day you are born and the day you find out why"

Mark Twain

What Is a Life Purpose?

Your Life Purpose is something that you want to create or contribute to throughout your life. It aligns with your values. In other words, it's something that means a lot to you, and you won't get tired of fulfilling it. Your Life Purpose is something that you can continue fulfilling throughout your entire life. It never runs out. It's not like a goal which has a deadline. It's not even quite like a mission, because a mission is really a large goal that can be completed. You might establish missions and goals which serve to fulfil your purpose, but your purpose is like an over-arching, guiding system to all that you do.

"Your purpose in life is to find your purpose and give your whole heart to it"

Buddha

Let's bring some clarity to this with an example. Let's take a man who must be one of the most prolific and long serving presenters of all time, Sir David Attenborough. Attenborough is a British Broadcaster and Natural Historian who has been presenting nature programmes for decades now. What's more, he's still going at the time of writing aged 95! Now, what keeps someone going all that time? One answer that might come to mind is **passion**. He certainly has tremendous passion for what he does. A person might say that it's his passion that has kept him going and who could disagree with this? It is his passion. He's taken his passion and done something with it; something **purposeful**. So, another key distinction is that you might have a passion; something you love and feel a great affinity towards, and you might use that to fulfil your purpose.

So, let's again look at Attenborough. If we were to say his purpose was 'to create a nature program', then we would be stating a goal and not a purpose. If we were to say his purpose was to create a series of nature programs, we could be stating a mission. If we said his purpose was to engage with his interest for the natural world, we would simply be stating a passion. So, what might his purpose be? I can only guess of course, but the following statements are more representative of a Life's Main Purpose.

> "To enable people to appreciate the beauty and wonder of the natural world"

Or perhaps a longer and more descriptive version might be…

"To educate people about the natural world so that they may have an enhanced appreciation for its wonder and beauty and an increased desire to preserve, protect and maintain it."

You may well have your own thoughts about what his purpose might be and how it might best be written, but hopefully these ideas give light to how a purpose is distinct from goals or even passions and how a purpose might be stated.

Long-time action film star Silvester Stallone, who gained great fame and acclaim from writing and starring in Rocky, apparently stated that his purpose has always been "to inspire people". If he had said his purpose was "to make movies" he would have been stating a mission or a goal. Many of his movies portray immense willpower and determination where his character comes up against the odds and keeps going no matter what. Stallone truly flies the flag for the values of courage, persistence and determination. Each movie acting as a vehicle to take him further on his journey to fulfilling his purpose of 'inspiring people'.

So, when writing a statement that best describes your purpose, it might be as short and concise as "to inspire people" or it may require more words to really contain what it is that you are wanting to do or express with your life. In the next few pages, I will guide you think about what your purpose might be and come up with your own written description.

Why Should You Discover Your Life's Main Purpose?

There are many great benefits to declaring to yourself a main purpose for your life. You will ignite a new lease of life inside yourself. You'll feel a sense of passion and confidence in yourself that you might not have felt before. It will positively energise you and have you feeling excited and happy more often.

Having a consciously driven purpose allows you to feel more engaged with life and more happy to be yourself. Your self-esteem will inevitably rise because you are indicating to yourself that you are a person with meaning in what you are and what you do. If you've tended to feel envious of others, your purpose will disengage you from those negative thoughts. You won't be concerned about comparing yourself with others; you'll wish others well and really mean it. You'll be able to celebrate other people's qualities and successes and feed from that energy. You'll better understand how you fit with the world and how things fit with you.

In short, knowing and engaging with your purpose will liberate and empower you and I urge you now to discover it. Answer the questions coming up and complete the process. Every second spent in this process is time well invested.

But...Do I Really Have a Purpose?

In the film Indiana Jones and The Last Crusade, Indiana is in pursuit of the Holy Grail. Held at gunpoint by the bad guys, he is forced to lead the way through a tunnel of deadly obstacles and finally arrives in the opening of a tomb which houses The Holy Grail. But The Grail is one among many chalices displayed there. The only way to know if you've chosen the right one, is to dip it in the holy water and drink from it. If you make the right choice, it gives you eternal life, but the wrong choice will take your life. The bad guy who has been close behind Indiana, steps onto the scene at this point and selects the most ornate looking cup. A gleaming golden chalice, studded with priceless jewels. On dipping it in the holy water and drinking, the bad guy quickly dies. Indiana then looks and selects the most ordinary looking chalice. A cup that's not shiny, not ornate. One made from clay. On drinking from it, he confirms that it is the real Holy Grail.

A person might think that their Life's Purpose must be something glamorous, spectacular and huge or it must mean they don't have one at all. They might think that one day it must occur to them in a special moment, like Moses standing on the hillside and God parting the waters to make obvious the way forward. I have heard people question and wonder whether they have a purpose and assume perhaps that if they did, surely life would have made it obvious to them by now. Some people may wonder if you're given a purpose in life or if you must make it up for yourself. And perhaps more people still never consider such things at all.

Whether your purpose occurs to you in a flash of insight, or it takes more thinking and pondering, does it really matter? I say, don't get hung up too much on the details. The questions coming up, especially when put together, are going to help to unlock key answers from your mind that have you think clearly and in the right way to identify what your life's purpose may be. You can start to explore options and say: then I think it might be this. Write that idea out and start to have it as a 'working statement' or 'statement in progress'. In time you might find yourself making small adjustments to it. Your purpose statement can evolve and adjust to feel increasingly right and true for you.

Your Quick Guide to Discovering Your Life's Main Purpose

The way to find an answer to something is to ask a question. This may sound obvious, but there are perhaps many times in life when we simply don't take the time to ask ourselves the questions needed to get the answers we want. The way to find a great answer is to ask a great question. Great questions are like the right keys to locked doors. Ask a great question, at the right moment and you might be surprised what is unlocked in your mind. Unlock one door and you might just start popping more and more open.

I call the following three questions Golden Questions, because they are really good ones to ask yourself. These questions will be enjoyable and productive for you to answer. They help you get to the core of what your life is really about. Take your time now and enjoy answering these questions. Your answers will reveal to you what you really want to do in and with your life.

GOLDEN QUESTION 1:

What have you always been trying to do with your life?

PROMPT:
Note the question; what have you been TRYING to do? What has really been your predominant intention

behind most of your actions and endeavours so far in life?

NOTE: If you just answer with: 'Get a good job' or 'Survive' or 'Escape' then you're too focused on moment-by-moment actions. If your answer isn't revealing, then ask yourself: What's behind that? I've been trying to do that in order for…what?

You might answer something like, to:

"Bring people together to increase peace & harmony"
"Help people to value the environment more"
"Help people to have greater health"
"Inspire people to be their best"
"Help animals and relieve any suffering"
"Relieve suffering in humans"
"Help people feel happy and free"
"Spread love and goodness to all"
"Master something so that I'm the best at it"

Notice that most of them mention other people, the environment or world around them. This is because a purpose spans beyond the individual and has a processional effect outward from them. A musician may be so engaged with their passion for their music, that it's only years later that they realise that their life has been serving the purpose of bringing people together in peace. An artist may just create their art as they engage with their passion and yet when other people express their appreciation of it, they realise that they've been serving a purpose they hadn't previously recognised. Even if a person is only aware that they just want to be the very best they can at something, that inevitably will have a positive knock-on effect to others. Perhaps that of inspiring others to be their best or helping others believe that they can do better at what they do. A purpose is about you, but it spreads beyond you. We're all part of this intricate human eco-system, aren't we? It fulfils you and serves the world around you at the same time. It's a natural win-win. A person may just be engaged with their passion, but don't you think the universe might have a bigger plan than a man or woman just doing something they like?

So, what have you always been trying to do with your life? If you haven't yet answered the question, go ahead and answer here.

....
....
....

Personally, throughout my life, I have always been trying to help people to feel good about themselves. This includes helping myself to feel good about me, because how can I help other people feel good if I don't? My wish is that through my words here I can pour, at least some of my life's good intentions towards you and facilitate you in having even greater rapport with yourself. I hope you do feel good about yourself and not just while reading this book, but increasingly more as you soon take action aligned with who you are. So, let's continue and explore you more.

GOLDEN QUESTION 2:

If you had all the money, all the resources and all the time you could ever need, what would you do?

PROMPT:

If your answer is to lie on a sofa watching Sports Centre with a can of beer and bowl of Doritos, then you haven't found your real purpose yet...keep going! If you come up with things like; go travelling or take loads of holidays, imagine you have had all the holiday you need and then return home fulfilled of that, THEN what would you do?

Write your answer below....

....
....
....
....
....
....
....
....
....

GOLDEN QUESTION 3:

When you're old, if you hadn't done it, what would you regret not doing with your life?

In order to answer this question, I want you to pause and imagine yourself many years in the future. Imagine being 'old you' and reflecting on your life. Once you've got your imagination going and you can sense being 'older you', then read the scenario below and answer the questions that follow:

SCENARIO...
You've done no more or less than what you've done so far in life. What are you proud of? What are you most happy about when considering the way you lived your life? However, what do you regret not doing with your life?

Write your answers below....

....
....
....
....
....
....

From these questions, now reflect and identify some key points. When answering what you regret not doing, think about this and start to recognise what things you desire to do in life that would really mean something to you. As the King of Personal Development; Anthony Robbins says, humans are really driven by two things: pain and pleasure. We can use our perception of future regrets to motivate us now. As mentioned, in part, this process is to help you bypass the limited thinking that tends to keep people coming back to patterns of familiarity in their day-to-day experience of life. Day to day and week to week, we may wave off opportunities and let things slip by all too easily. However, using retrospection (looking back in time) we can shift our perceptions and create a sense of urgency or higher value on choices in the now. We tip the threshold point of perceived pain and say: no matter what courage **it seems** to require of me now in this moment, it is **less** painful for me to take that action now, than the pain of regretting inaction later. Without this counterbalance of future pain, we may be all too happy to drift along the path of least resistance. We procrastinate and fall prey to 'manana' thinking ('tomorrow' in Spanish). Manana, manana…. I will do my thing tomorrow. Soon we find that thousands of 'mananas' have come and gone, and we still haven't done our thing!

So, if you haven't done it yet, take a short time to imagine the scenario above and answer the questions. As you imagine stepping into 'older you', allow yourself to feel your feelings as if you really are there in the future, looking back on your life. It's when you tap these emotions that you activate a type of intelligence that can guide you to adjust the course of your life now. Feel that regret for what you never got around to doing. We want to get you in the present moment to a point of emotional breakthrough, where any fears of the actions you might need to take dissolve by comparison to living with this regret. Really imagine sitting there as old you, regretting. Not having any power to change things. Thinking "if only I had"…… Feel the pain of that powerlessness to act or do anything different and let it ignite within you the realisation of opportunity that you really do have now.

Creating Your Purpose Statement

So, what have you learned about yourself from these three golden questions? What insights have you had? Whatever has occurred to you, you're now going to bring things together by creating a concise but powerful statement of your intention.

Use the below guide as a template for an initial draft purpose statement. This initial statement is more complete and complex than what you will end up with, but it helps guide you to get three big things in: The 'Wow' (line 1), the 'How' (line 2) and the 'Why' (line 3). On line 1, knowing yourself now, write what your instincts tell you that you think your main purpose might be. Keep it generalised on this line, for example: help people be… (healthy/happy/confident, etc…) OR improve the environment, OR make life better for (children, adults with……., animals, etc). On line 2, just start to add a little about what you might be doing to accomplish this. Sprinkling a little of the practical in helps make it real. Finally on line 3, bring forward some of your core values. Which of your values would doing this fulfil the most? Putting these in make it even more emotive to you.

So, go ahead now and fill in your draft purpose.

DRAFT PURPOSE STATEMENT:

1. My purpose is to

   ..………………………………………...………….

   …………………………………………………..………

   …………………………………………………………..

2. By doing

   …………...…………………………………...………

   …………………………………………..……………

   ………………………………………………....……..

3. Which fulfils my values of

   ……………………………………………..…………

   ……………………………………………..…………

   ……………………………………………..…………

Now you have a choice:

1. You're happy with it.
If your purpose statement looks great to you and feels compelling, then you have it and it's done. You might like to create another copy of it and display it somewhere you'll see it often.

2. It could be better.
Keep re-working it until it starts to feel and look and sound more concise and compelling to you.

3. More Concise.
If you'd like a more concise version, then you can now simply remove lines 2 and 3. Doing the 3-line version first was worth it because you can check whether it fits together well. Does it appeal to your core values? Does it seem like you have the right interests and skills or ones that you can develop?

My suggestion is that you create and display both versions of your purpose statement. The 3-line version and the more concise line 1 only version. Jot these into a journal or diary or desktop place where you will naturally remind yourself of them. Think regularly of your concise version and drill it in your mind. You will start to notice yourself accomplishing your purpose at moments when in the past, you may have been unaware of yourself. This just means from now on, you can have an enhanced appreciation of yourself and what will this do for your self-esteem, your happiness and the quality of your life?

"There is no greater gift you can give or receive than to honour your calling. It's why you were born and how you can become the most truly alive"

Oprah Winfrey

Your Personality

"Beauty captures the eye, but personality captures the heart"

Oscar Wilde

Nobody knows you like you do. You know your preferences for foods, music, sleep times, hobbies and interests, your habits, your strengths and weaknesses, your hopes and fears. You've lived with yourself every moment of your life; you know what you're like. So, what's the chances of something outside of you helping you to know yourself any better? Well, I have a key question for you:

Is being accustomed to yourself the same as knowing yourself?

You might have had the experience of hearing yourself on a recording and thinking, "I don't sound like that, do I?!" ....or seeing yourself on video and thinking "That's not how I move and look, is it?" And, in a similar way, exploring the qualities of your personality can hold up a mirror to your character and allow you to reflect from an outside perspective. It might help you gain objective thoughts which support your decision making about what you are best suited to.

I believe a personality trait is like a piece of a far larger puzzle. Imagine a puzzle with a background perhaps of the ocean or sky. Some pieces bring with them foreground information with colourful images and dimensions. Other pieces have less colour and more background. Profiling yourself by identifying certain traits is like putting on the table some of the pieces that make up your entirety; the ones with the most colour. Those pieces are useful to look at because they seem to have the most information about you, but bear in mind they are not the complete picture. You are always more than what's contained in a few pieces.

Definitions

In their book: 'Theories of Personality', Jess and Gregory Feist give the following definition of what personality is:

> "Traits and characteristics that give both consistency and individuality to a person's behaviours."

The American Dictionary's definition is:

> "The special combination of qualities in a person that makes that person different from others, as shown by the way the person behaves, feels and thinks."

Both definitions highlight individuality don't they? You might think of your personality as a range of qualities which allow you to be unique. The Feist's definition includes consistency. Your personality will tend to keep you consistent in your behaviours. If you did something others don't identify with you, they might remark that it was "out of character". If you display behaviours consistently, others will tend to think, "yep, that's Jill for you...that's what she's like" or "yes, that's Bill, he's a good guy".

How do astronomers identify stars? They may endeavour to tell them apart by size, distance, brightness, colour tints, movement speeds and maybe other factors. The astronomer might zoom in to see the details of each star and when they zoom out they are reminded that they are part of a far wider and more complex constellation. In the same way, we will 'zoom in' on some of your 'traits'. They can reveal certain insights about yourself. Like a constellation of stars, your qualities somehow fit together, draw on each other and create the magnificent uniqueness of yourself. Every constellation of stars is somewhat different, some with higher density of stars in certain places and some with stars further away from the centre. Humans can have many similar traits, but never the identical same distinctions in totality.

Influences and Changes

While your attitudes and beliefs about yourself are likely to adapt and change, your personality will stay with you throughout your life. Your personality traits have a permanence to them which makes them worth knowing. This is not to say that someone doesn't mature and change in certain ways. It doesn't mean you'll laugh at the same things when you are 20 as you did when you were 10. Of course, your tastes and preferences for things adapt and change, but at a deep level of personality, you don't. If you were agreeable and conscientious as a teenager, it's unlikely you'd become disagreeable and low in conscientiousness in your 30's or 40's or even your 60's.

You represent your personality through your actions, choices, mannerisms, and behaviours. What you do and the way you do it. What you say and the way you say it. It makes you unique and allows other people to know how they want to be connected with you. We might think it's other people's influence that determines what we're like, but we may feel drawn towards them because of how we already are. We feel the connection due to something inside of ourselves.

The Myers Briggs Type Indicator

Extensive efforts have been made to categorise human personality, usually by identifying our various qualities, more often referred to as our 'traits'. Full books have been written on personality, but here I will endeavour to give you a concise awareness of some of these categorisations to see if you can gain further useful insights about yourself.

For many decades now, Myers Briggs Personality Indicators have been widely used by organisations, in an attempt to predict which person is best suited to which job role. The Myers Briggs system facilitates an assessment around 4 key 'types'. Essentially 4 traits played off against what was chosen as their opposite trait. As person is...

Extraverted [E] OR Introverted [I]
Sensing [S] OR INtuitive [N]
Feeling [F] OR Thinking [T]
Perceiving [P] OR Judging [J]

Now, even as you look at these, you might already be thinking that you are not wholly just one or other of these, but remember the process of labelling with traits is like zooming in on one star in a constellation. It's useful to zoom in sometimes, but then zoom out again and put it in context. Take what's useful to you, you might gain some helpful nudges of insight and awareness.

Your Turn...

So, take a moment to consider these for yourself; are you more Extraverted, which means outwardly focused on the world around you, or Introverted, which means more inclined to reflect inwardly on your own thoughts and ideas? Are you more Sensing, which means judging things by your senses moment to moment (things that seem factual) or are you more Intuitive, which means judging more by instinct and possibility; things which seem like they are possible even if not sensed yet? Are you more of a Feeler, responding to situations more by your feelings, or a Thinker; more emotionally cool and instead looking for the facts? Finally, are you more of a Perceiver, open to forming new perceptions of things, or a Judger; who likes to have things settled and pre-determined? Again, if you have it, release the tension in your mind telling you that you're not just one and not the other of these.

Go with what side of the spectrum you veer towards more.

The final task here is to create your sequence of letters. If you are more Extraverted, then give yourself the letter 'E' or if you are more Introverted then give yourself the letter 'I'. Then an 'S' for Sensing or an 'N' for Intuitive, an 'F' for Feeling or 'T' for Thinking and finally a P for Perceiving or give yourself a J if you are more Judging. This then labels your identified 'type'. So, you might be an 'ENFP', that's Extravert, Intuitive, Feeling, Perceiving. Or you might be an 'ISTJ', that's Introvert, Sensing, Thinking, Judging and so on. Hopefully you get the idea. So go ahead and create your 4-letter sequence now.

At the time of my writing this book, there's a great website called 16personalities.com which allows you to go further with this Myers Briggs system and identify your lead traits. If you are interested, I recommend visiting it and allowing it to help guide you to determine your Myers Briggs indicator.

The Enneagram Model

Another popular model is called the Enneagram of Personality. In this model, you distinguish your 'type' from a choice of 9. The Type 1 person is 'The Moral Perfectionist', a person with high ideals and standards. Type 2 is 'The Helper', a person who is compassionate, generous and friendly. Type 3 is 'The Achiever', driven and ambitious. Type 4 is 'The Romantic' who likes to express passion and sensitivity. Type 5 is 'The Investigator', with strong analytical skills, they like to find out how things work. Type 6 is 'The Loyal Guardian' who is loyal, likeable and reliable but guarded and sceptical. Type 7 is 'The Optimist', who is enthusiastic and fun loving. Type 8 is 'The Protector', resilient and strong in protecting their values. And finally, Type 9, 'The Peacekeeper', a person who is open-minded and generous and doesn't mind mediating people rather than being in the spotlight.

Again, I am only touching briefly on this here and you may wish to do your own research. But for now, perhaps as you read this through, you had thoughts about yourself and which 'type' reflected you best. Maybe there are several 'types' who's qualities somewhat represent you and how you are. However, temporarily narrowing your focus in on one 'type' that perhaps best represents you could be useful. This 'label' is restrictive and doesn't represent ALL of your qualities, but, if there was one 'type' from the Enneagram that stood out the most for you, which would it be? Take a moment to consider this.

The Big Five

One further model was initiated by the works of psychologists in the 1930's and 40's and continued to evolve. This evolution involved condensing a large number of personality factors down to just 5 core traits that all humans have to varying degrees. These became known as the 'Big 5', finalised by Fiske, Norman, Smith, Goldberg, McCrea and Costa. They determined that the essence of your personality can be identified when looking at the following traits:

Openness. How open are you to new experiences? How much do you naturally like to engage with the world around you and feel happy to try new things?

Conscientiousness. To what extent do you feel driven to stay with tasks and reliably work at things? Do you have a strong sense of duty and of what's right?

Extraversion. Do you feel positive and energised in groups and relish social interactions? Do you like lots of social interaction and stimulation?

Agreeableness. Do you have high levels of tolerance and patience with people? How willing are you to adapt and accommodate in order to get on well with others?

Neuroticism. Do you tend to get anxious or feel stressed and on edge easily? Do you have regular mood swings?

Your Turn again…
Have a look at the illustration below and rate yourself on each trait by drawing a cross on the line at a point which represents you best.

The Big 5
Personality Traits

Cut the line where you think represents you for each trait

Openness
Low ─────────────────────── High

Conscientiousness
Low ─────────────────────── High

Extraversion
Low ─────────────────────── High

Agreeableness
Low ─────────────────────── High

Neuroticism
Low ─────────────────────── High

Now step back and think about what you might have just learned about yourself.

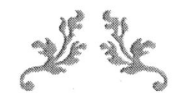

"Your personality creates your personal reality"

Joe Dispenza

How does your personality affect your life?

Your personality is somewhat etched into your neurology and biological systems and is going to have at least some effect on how you think and respond. Someone who is highly extraverted is more likely to show excitement in public, where someone more Introverted would likely have a more contained response. Someone highly conscientious feels compelled to wash those dishes right away, where someone lower in conscientiousness is ok with leaving them. Your personality will influence not only your personal actions, but also who you feel more connected to and compelled to align with.

Career Decisions

The popularity of personality scales show a strong consensus in the value of knowing yourself when considering your career or job role. What could you learn about yourself from your analysis of the Big 5? Are you very open? Then maybe you'd thrive in the kind of work that allows you to experience a variety of places, people and situations. Start to think and make a list of options. If you are less open, you might be more suited to work that has more established rituals and routines.

Are you highly conscientious? If so, think about what role you might like to take on. Perhaps you can be happy taking a high level of responsibility. Maybe as a manager, owner or other type of leader. Other people will benefit from your reliability and work ethic and you might want to ensure that you are valued and rewarded for it. If you feel you are less conscientious and instead more 'easy going', you might look to find a type of work where you have more choices that suit you and less pressure to perform to deadlines.

Are you highly extraverted? If so, you might be of great service in a customer facing role or one where you make presentations to potential customers or groups. You might enjoy work that opens opportunities to meet new people or host or lead groups. If you are more introverted, you might have an advantage of being able to stay focused on more solitary tasks better; quietly progressing on your own accord. Again start to think and list what options come to mind.

If you are highly agreeable, you might be able to get on well with prospective customers and build trust with potential alliances. You might like to pursue work in teaching or guiding and helping people and you're likely to work well in teams. If you feel you are lower on the agreeableness spectrum, you might prefer work which requires less dependence on personal interactions. Equally, if you are quite neurotic, you might choose to stay out of high pressure jobs and find what allows you to relax more and be clear about your tasks and expectations.

These are generalisations and I encourage you to think more about what would suit and fulfil you the most. As mentioned earlier in this book, rather than worrying about where you fit, think about what fits you. Start with these understandings of yourself and allow your mind to explore options.

Relationships

As I'm sure you can imagine, your personality has a significant influence on your relationships. Likewise, the personalities of your friends, love partner and other people you spend your time with, matter to you. If you are high in conscientiousness and you live with someone at the other end of the spectrum, well, good luck with that! You might have a few issues with who's done or not done the dishes! The conscientious house mate can't stand the mess and the less conscientious house mate can't understand why the other can't just "chill out more".

Another tricky match up might come about if you are highly open and you have a relationship with someone far more closed. You might want to travel and explore places, while they prefer to stay in and have a quieter routine. You might want to do things in your life that you feel you couldn't do with this person by your side. If you are extraverted and they are introverted, you might want to host great parties and meet with groups of friends, where they would prefer individual interactions. If you are highly agreeable but they don't tend to trust or get on so well with people as you do, you might feel embarrassed or frustrated by your less flourishing social life. If they are far more neurotic than you, you might struggle to empathise.

Conclusions

In writing this chapter on personality, my intention has been to get you thinking objectively about yourself and others. Hopefully you've gained one or two extra understandings which can help you nudge your decision making to work better for you over time. Take moments to consider what new decisions or adjustments you could make to give yourself more chance of flourishing, both in your career and relationships. Equally, I hope this knowledge allows you a little more capacity for tolerance and appreciation; the understandings needed to relate effectively with yourself and others. If you feel, through this knowledge, you have a fraction more of this then, happily, I have achieved my objective. Now, with your increased self-awareness, let's move on to the subject of knowing what you want.

"Your personality is a tool for your soul"

Gary Zukav

PART 2

What do you want?

Here in Part 2, you are going to gain more awareness about what you really want in life. The chapters here present you an opportunity to consider yourself in the light of three key areas: Your Emotional Needs, Your Feelings and your Decisions.

These understandings will help you ensure that you balance your choices in ways that allow you to feel complete, fulfilled and happy in life. If you only go for something because it makes you money, without consideration for your needs and the feelings you want to experience, then you might pay an unnecessarily high price to gain that money. What if, all along, there was a way to make great money while enjoying life a whole lot more? Therefore, a way which was more sustainable and allowed you to feel more balanced, satisfied and true to yourself.

Now with your already greater awareness of your values, personality and purpose, this part is here to facilitate your thinking of how best to decide what you really want in life. Such decision making can be a bit like panning for gold. You may need to sift through thoughts and ideas until the right ones shine through.

Your Needs

"Human hopes and human creeds, have their roots in human needs"

Eugene Fitch Ware

Something else that's worthy of your awareness and attention are your Human Emotional Needs. Sometimes referred to as your: 'Emotional Needs' or 'Human Needs' or just 'Needs'. Whatever the label given, it's key to understand that you have needs in your life. Yes, I do mean 'needs' as opposed to just 'wants'. These needs are within you and influence you whether you are aware of them or not.

It's important to know what needs you have and how they influence you because, whatever you endeavour to achieve, if you neglect your needs, you're unlikely to feel as you want to feel, regardless of achievement. You might have a strong intention to stay with a plan of action, but if it takes you away from the fulfilment of your needs too much, there may come a point where you find yourself sabotaging your results. Bear in mind and remember, if you have an unhappy internal system running the show; the show is unlikely to go well. On making decisions about what you want in life and setting up ways to achieve that, keep in mind the needs that I present to you in this chapter.

Contributors to Our Understandings

Human Needs have been studied by some emanant people in the field of psychology. Perhaps most well-known is Abraham Maslow, an American Psychologist who created Maslow's Hierarchy of Human Needs. You might know it as Maslow's Pyramid because, to illustrate this hierarchy, he presented a pyramid with 5 levels.

The base level represents Physiological Needs; the need to breathe, drink, eat, sleep and maintain a good temperature. The second level up represents Safety; the need to avoid danger and have a secure environment. The third level represents Love and Belonging; the need for love, intimacy, family and friendship. The fourth level up represents Self Esteem; the need for a sense of achievement, worth and recognition. Finally, the fifth level represents what Maslow termed 'Self-Actualisation'. By this he meant living to the best of our abilities and fulfilling our potential.

Other mentionable people of influence are Ivan Tyrell and Joe Griffin, founders of 'Human Givens Theory' and Anthony Robbins, a force of nature in the world of Personal Development. Both parties lay out their version of needs, both with credibility behind them and apparent good sense. What's more, it's re-assuring that both their versions and Maslow's Pyramid seem to me to have crossovers which support the validity of the other. Feel free to do your own research if you want, but for now, rather than regurgitating them to you here, I would prefer to save you time and condense them into the essence of what I believe you need to take away from this chapter. The following is my interpretation, taken from studies of these respected sources and condensed for your convenience.

Here's what I suggest will serve you best in your awareness. You have the following needs in your life.

The Need For...

1. Safety and Security....(a sense that you can rely on certain things around you)

2. Connection ....(love, intimacy, attention, friendship and connection with a wider community)

3. Significance (a sense that you matter and have value to the world around you)

4. Competence (a sense of challenge which expands your abilities and enhances your self-esteem)

5. Purpose and Fulfilment (a sense of meaning and contribution)

So, as you think about what you want and start to make decisions and set goals, bear in mind your need for each of these aspects in your life. I'm sure you've read or heard many times that balance is a key thing in life. Well, here it is again, that same old message. Deciding what you want in life is best done with an acute awareness of what you also need, so that you can balance and fulfil both. Both your wants and your needs. Neglect of needs is likely to pull you off focus anyway and have you feeling less than your best. And if you're feeling less than your best, how can you do your best?

How Your Needs Affect Your Behaviours

If a person is 'acting up' it could signify a need of theirs being unmet. Think of your own behaviours in life so far. Have you had moments where your behaviour surprised or even disturbed you? It could be that someone strongly violated one of your core values, but it also may have been that you were not getting a need met. Your behaviours will reflect your level of need fulfilment as well as some of the other aspects we're looking at in this book.

Safety

If a person doesn't feel safe, it's hard for them to do anything but attend to the responses and behaviours they perceive will keep them safe. If a person doesn't feel safe and secure in an environment they are working in, how likely are they to be at their best? Think of Maslow's Pyramid again, safety is the near the base. Until someone has this in place, it's hard for them to move up to higher levels of functioning and fulfilment. Your brain will operate on handling what's known moment to moment, rather than opening more creative faculties. They might retract and shut down for fear of doing something wrong. On the flip side, if a person feels safe and secure with you or in an environment you're helping to create, they will have the chance of moving up in the quality of actions and responses. If they feel supported and assured in themselves, it's far more likely they will tap into their more creative faculties and start to thrive.

Connection

If a person's need for connection is attended to, they will tend to feel accepted, liked and valued. Their nurtured sense of connection will inevitable have a positive cross-over effect also into other needs. As they feel more connected, they feel more secure, safe and happy. How might this person behave? Perhaps with a positive hora of self-assurance? Whereas a person who is not meeting their need for connection may behave in ways that show greater need for other people's approval of them or 'neediness'.

Significance

Significance is a need that people may accomplish by a variety of behaviours. A person is far better aligned in their choices and actions if they can fulfil their need for significance through positive means. If you believe in the work you do in life and feel recognised for your value, this may add many credits to your significance account. If a person's significance account is bankrupt, you might expect some negative compensatory behaviours to come. If a person holds a gun to your head and starts giving you commands, that will give them an instant boost in significance, won't it? After all, they have certainly become significant to you! Another negative attempt to fill the need may be through pulling others down. Within significance comes a sense of respect and attention and some people start a gang or cult where they look to dominate. And so, if a person fails to find a positive way to feel significant, they might find a short-cut through a negative way instead.

Competence and Purpose

There's a saying; "if you're not growing…you're dying" and it's important to recognise that a continuation of challenge and engagement of abilities is important at any stage of life. A person might look forward to retirement and yet, when they get there, suffer from a sense of stagnancy and lack of growth. This need for competence coincides somewhat with the need for purpose and fulfilment and when a person identifies an ongoing life purpose, there's always more for them to do and to become. So, it's a key thing to remember to stretch yourself in certain interests, contributions and endeavours, whatever they are for you. Not stress yourself, but happily, stretch yourself. Engage in life and fulfil yourself; it's in your DNA to do so!

Now Rate Yourself

So, as you consider your life, think about these five areas of need and take a moment to rate yourself. On a scale of 0-10, if a 0 is akin to a bankrupt account and a 10 is as full as you would like it to be, how are you presently scoring in each need area?

How would you rate yourself for your present fulfilment level of safety and security? How safe and secure do you feel? Hopefully that one is quite high for you. If you'd say it's below a 7, perhaps there are some key changes you want to make as a point of priority.

What about connection? Go with your instinct and give yourself a present rating. Bear in mind we may have many ways of feeling connected. Connection can be with animals, nature and the planet and universe as well as other people. Many people love owning pets or find that hiking in nature enhances their sense of connection to the world around them. Other people might gain this from participating in hobbies or supporting a sports team or from spiritual engagements.

What about significance? Rate yourself for that too. How much do you feel you get acknowledged? Do you feel you gain a sense of significance through your career or from being a parent or friend or being really good at something? Or do you feel that this is a need that you struggle to get fulfilled? Again, rate it from 0-10 with 10 being as fulfilled as you would like to feel in this area.

Consider next your sense of competence for various pursuits and endeavours in your life. My take on this is; rather than judging your abilities, instead rate yourself based on how fulfilled your need for a sense of competence is. You might have only just started some pursuits and so you cannot expect mastery yet. But how much do you feel you are fulfilling your need for getting good at things of interest to you? Are you growing? Are you challenging yourself and expanding your abilities? Just being engaged in pursuits that can lead to competence later increases your fulfilment in this area.

Finally, rate yourself for your need to feel purposeful in your life. How much do you feel like your life has meaning and purpose? We gain this through our choice of work or by having children and the way we are with family and friends. We can gain purposefulness by being active within a community. We can feel purposeful in life through pursuits and contributions. Perhaps the best thing, and hopefully you've done this already in Part 1, is to define for yourself a main purpose in life. This allows you to consciously direct your choices and actions so that you can fulfil your need at the highest level.

Take Away's

So, what could you take with you from this chapter? Do you have any needs that could do with some extra attention? Are you connecting with others and the world around you enough and following pursuits which have meaning and purpose for you? You may have concluded that you'll need to take all sorts of action, but in reality, you might find that increasing your sense of fulfilment for one need just takes one or two actions. In turn, this is likely to have a positive knock-on effect in other areas. One of the great things about being a human, is that our well-being is like an eco-system, things are connected. And if you make a positive difference in just one area, it's likely to spill over into other areas.

So I'd like to encourage you to choose just one thing, but then really commit to doing it. Choose one need which you want to fulfil more and then answer this question:

What ONE thing could you do which, if you did it, would bring a rise in fulfilment to this need? Then do that.

Keep these needs in mind as you progress on in life and bear them in mind for other people around you. It's likely now that you'll be able to identify times where another person is 'acting up' or behaving strange. Is someone trying to gain significance by dominating others or using negative behaviours? Hopefully you can sense that through the processes in this book, you're gaining awareness of what will bring you a sense of significance but by positive means and competence fulfilled by taking action to achieve this. My belief is that the more we can help ourselves in life, the better we can support and help others. So, let's keep progressing on and next we come to your decisions.

"When people appear to be something other than good and decent, it is only because they are reacting to deprivation of basic human needs"

Abraham Maslow

Your Decisions

"Good decisions come from experience. Experience comes from making bad decisions"

Mark Twain

You've come to a point where you know your values, your needs and you're getting clearer about your Life Purpose. The good news now is that you can use this awareness to guide your decisions. Knowing these things is akin to knowing what your body needs for good health. In the same way that you can walk around a supermarket making good choices, you can now walk around the supermarket of life…making good choices. With self-clarity, decisions become easier.

Fitting In

It was the year 2001. I remember visiting my University's Career Advice Centre, hoping for some guidance in my decisions, but instead being handed a stack of booklets and an A-Z list of hundreds of jobs. I remember the empty, sinking feeling I had as I read through a vast list of jobs that I had no interest in doing. A year later I went travelling round the world, "to find myself" of course. But it turned out I wasn't on the other side of the planet either!

I have found that you do not get to know what you want in life without a process of asking yourself good questions, reflecting on them and making decisions.

From a process of self-reflection and thinking, you can bring yourself to clarity. This self-knowledge allows you to flip things around. Where, without it, you are at the effect of the world around you and need to see where you can 'fit in', with it, you can take life on and see 'what fits you'.

Without self-awareness, it's too easy to persuade ourselves into thinking we have more limited choices than we do and that we are better off staying with something that's already familiar to us. It's human nature to take the path of least resistance, but it might end up being the path of least fulfilment. If you are serious about your happiness and fulfilment (and you are by the way because you're reading this book), then you must also be serious about being willing to make decisions. It's only through decisions that you can take charge and consciously direct your life. And there's no escape by the way, even indecision gives you decisions; "Do I get on the ship or stay on the shore?". And, as you stand there deliberating…you watch it sail away. There we go; your decision made for you!

The purpose of this chapter is to help you enhance your confidence in making decisions and release some of the perceived stress that you might have around them. It's time to step into your decision-making shoes and then walk boldly forwards.

Your Ability To Decide

You are an expert decision maker. How do I know this? Because you make thousands of decisions every day, you just don't realise it. You wake up and decide; how to get out of bed, whether to have a drink, what to wear, what to eat, where to stand, where to sit, how fast or slow to move and how to respond to things around you. You're constantly making decisions. If you doubt your decision-making abilities, just look around your home and notice the thousands of decisions you've made. Clothes, books, gadgets, furniture, decorations and ornaments. What areas to leave more open and where to place your things. What to throw out, what to keep and where to store them. All decisions you've been perfectly capable of making. Even some of the decisions you think you didn't make were a decision not to decide.

Taking The Pressure Off

Coming back to Indiana Jones and the Last Crusade. At one point, when Indiana is passing through that tunnel of deadly challenges to get to the Holy Grail, he comes to a great deep opening in the ground in front of him, with no way to pass. A giant crevasse that would take his life. However, in front of him lies an invisible bridge, unseen to his eyes and one that will only appear if he believes it is there. And he must not tip toe out either or it won't appear, he must boldly step out and trust that it exists. He must take a 'leap of faith'.

Some decisions may seem to require a leap of faith on your part. You may not be able to know what lies ahead until you step forwards. Like climbing a mountain, you take the equipment you believe you need and trust you will find a way, but it's only as you climb that the mountain reveals the way forward. It's unlikely that many decisions in life will require you to risk falling. Some may require you to risk sliding back somewhat, but not a complete fall. Yet it's perhaps too easy to treat decisions this way. What if I get it wrong? What if?! And there it is, right there! Survival mode kicks in and snubs out our modern drive for fulfilment. Seeing decisions as potentially fatal leaps stops a human in their tracks and keeps them hallucinating negative scenarios. As Shakespeare says in Hamlet; thinking makes cowards of us all.

So, on this topic of seeing decisions as risks that we fear to make in case we get it wrong, let's break this down and come right back to the original intention of the word decision. The Latin root of the word decision is 'to cut'. So, rather than thinking of decisions as terminal acts that you must get right, think of them as part of a process of cutting down variables. From a number of options, you may need to keep cutting down until you gain the awareness that culminates in the best outcomes for you. Essentially, don't be afraid to decide. Decisions lead to revelations. They offer you the chance to learn from new experience that you wouldn't have otherwise had.

Motivational speaker, Brian Tracy talks about something he calls 'Zero Based Thinking'. This is where once in a while; you stop and ask yourself...

> "Knowing what I now know, is what I've decided on still the best choice?"

He says you should always permit yourself to change your mind based on new knowledge. Knowledge which helps you to continue to 'cut', to make new decisions.

Tracy also shares a great metaphor for how life really works. He says, life unveils the truth to you only when you are willing to take the next step forwards. This is where the modern person must drive through and bypass those old survival mechanisms. The ones that try to persuade us to stay with what's familiar, for fear of the unknown. I doubt you will be chased by predators or fall down any crevasses! Brian Tracy says; imagine life holds a curtain up in front of you. When you step up to the curtain, life will then step back and reveal your next options. Step up again and life will reveal the next series of opportunities for you. But life will never show you the full picture at the beginning of any endeavour. If you are unwilling to step up and try things despite uncertainty, then you will never get to see the next part of the journey and certainly not the end.

"In any moment of decision, the best thing you can do is the right thing, the next best thing is the wrong thing, and the worst thing you can do is nothing"

Theodore Roosevelt

The Gift and Curse of Modern Times

As we entered the industrial revolution and more recently the technological revolution, our choices started to increase in the developed world. A person of average salary today has almost immediate access to luxuries that even a King or Queen a few hundred years ago could only dream of. Humanity in the developed countries may have made the assumption that our happiness would reflect that. Surely having more choices would always be better than fewer? What do you think?

The curious thing, in my opinion, is that increased choice doesn't seem to increase happiness by default. Not by any means. We seem to have happy rich people and miserable rich people, happy poor people and miserable poor people. More choices could be great for one person but could lead another into an endless loop of distraction, pulling them away from what's more important. This could be the best time ever to live or maybe the most overwhelming and confusing time. What we need, and perhaps more than ever, is a highly developed inner guidance system. One which can keep us balanced and aware.

Your Inner Guidance System

Your values have been guiding you throughout your life already and making many decisions seem easy. You didn't hit that person in the face because you have the value of peace or respect. You didn't rob that bank or get into drug dealing because honesty and integrity are values you hold. You were polite and pleasant to all those people because you value: connection, tolerance, peace and harmony. An unconsciously established system of values, operating in the background of your awareness, unseen, but very much there.

The clearer your values, the easier many decisions become. You gain a clearer sense of: how to respond to people and the things that happen, what to say and do or what to avoid. The clearer your values, the more assured you feel in your choices, knowing what's right for you. The clearer your values, the easier it is to be ok with your decisions and content within yourself as you look back on them. So be sure soon and ideally regularly, to go back to your list of core values and drive them more deeply into your awareness.

As well as your values, allow your needs and your purpose to guide you. When faced with an important choice, ask yourself:

"Which option fulfils my values, needs and purpose best?"

A Great Question to Ask Yourself

Go ahead now and make a decision to do something by answering the following question.

QUESTION:

What ONE thing, if I was to do it, would make the greatest positive difference to my life at the present time?

Write your answer down and take action on it as soon as possible.

Decision Making Tools

MORE, LESS, STOP, START QUADRANTS

One decision making tool which can focus your mind on making improvements is called 'More, Less, Stop, Start'. Simply draw out four quadrants by drawing a giant plus sign on a page and title them: More, Less, Stop, Start. Then use each quadrant to list ideas of things that come to mind. Thinking of what you want or alternatively, what would bring you greater productivity, ask yourself:

What do I want to do:

More of? Less of? Start doing? And to Stop doing?

Fill out your quadrants with the ideas that come to mind.

This simple exercise helps you to gain clarity about your priorities and can spark new motivation to adjust your actions.

BEST, WORST, LIKELY CASE SCENARIOS

Another simple decision-making tool which you may have heard of, is simply to run through in your mind, or on paper, what might be the best, worst or most likely outcomes of any decision. If you have an important decision to make and you're not sure how to decide, by writing out your answers to these three scenarios honestly, it can help you to reach a point of decision with more certainty. When you see the worst-case scenario written down, you might think to yourself; "You know what…I can even handle that" or you might realise "wow that would be really bad, it's not worth the risk!". Here's a few examples:

SCENARIO 1: Should I walk up to Rosie and ask her out?

Worst Case: She rejects me loudly, her friends laugh, and I look stupid and feel bad.

Likely Case: She says she has a boyfriend.

Best Case: She says yes!

DECISION: Do It! It's totally worth the risk. If the worst case happens, I can deal with it.

SCENARIO 2: Should I take drugs with those guys when we go out tonight?

Worst Case: I have a terrible reaction which I never fully recover from and maybe get arrested in connection with drugs.

Likely Case: I will get away with it and feel a bit high and then feel rubbish tomorrow.

Best Case: I will get a real high and feel great.

DECISION: Don't do it! The worst-case scenario is so bad and leads to long term consequences for the sake of a really short-term pleasure.

SCENARIO 3: Should I apply for the new job?

Worst Case: I don't get it and I feel frustrated and like I wasted a day of my time.

Likely Case: I narrowly miss out, but they know I'm keen to take on a higher job role.

Best Case: I get it and get a pay rise, a job I prefer to do and feel really good about myself!

DECISION: Do it! There's so much to gain and really nothing to lose.

Final Thoughts

And so, as you step forwards with faith, do you need the faith that you'll make perfect decisions? No! More like the faith that you can positively learn from and respond to anything. As you trust yourself to run with your decisions, life will unveil the next pieces, just as a mountain reveals its paths as you climb. You only have to commit to the climb, not the route.

Take these understandings inside yourself. It's going to seem like some decisions you make are good and some are bad, but as long as you are guided by your internal system of values, needs and purpose, all decisions take you closer to what you want. Your main decision is which mountain to conquer, not the details of the route up it. You don't get to see these things until you step forwards to life and say: "I'm here.... I'm ready, bring it on!" Staying open to new understandings and making new decisions based on them, is the very essence of good decision making. Don't be afraid to step back sometimes and ask yourself: "knowing what I now know...is this still the best way forward?" Knowing that you can trust yourself to adapt as you go, will help you to be bold and step up to life more often. And, as you do so, life has no choice but to unveil to you the truths you seek.

"May your choices reflect your hopes,
not your fears"

Nelson Mandela

Your Feelings

"Nothing is either good or bad but thinking makes it so"

William Shakespeare (Hamlet)

What you really want in life is feelings. That's right, FEELINGS. You are driven towards the actions and behaviours that you THINK will bring you the feelings you want. As Personal Development legend Anthony Robbins says, we're driven away from pain and towards pleasure. At least, what we PERCEIVE will bring us pain or pleasure. There's another level at play here too. We play off the two, knowing that in order to ultimately have what we want, we often have to go through enough of what we don't want first. A person may not love the moments where they are pushing themselves hard at exercise, but they are willing to do it for the good feelings they have about themselves later. A person may not like the early starts, but they will get to work and discipline themselves to do the hard stuff, because they tell themselves it'll be worth it. Besides, how much pain will they have if they lose their job and end up bankrupt!

"Discipline weighs ounces and regret weighs tonnes"

Jim Rohn

Think about it. Why does anyone really do anything? Why do people give their time to helping others? Why do we want nice cars, nice clothes? Why would someone put the effort into creating a beautiful home or garden or a work of art? Because we want to feel something. We want to feel good about ourselves. We want to involve ourselves with things and have things that help us trigger good feelings in ourselves. We want to feel loved, accepted, cherished and needed. We want to feel valued and appreciated, accomplished and successful. We want to feel like we can create things and make a difference, like we matter, like we belong and like we're connected. These feelings are what we are all after and we all have our various ways of trying to get them. Some people through mastering skills or creating things, others through material wealth or by travelling the world, others more through building friendships or hosting social gatherings and so on. Some people will gain feelings by throwing themselves off tall buildings with a parachute or bungee rope. Other people will attempt to gain the feelings they seek by overeating, smoking, drinking too much or taking drugs. Realise, all of our behaviours are driven by the desire for feelings.

Think Good to Feel Good

The key to feeling good is thinking good. This may sound far too simple, but it is profoundly true. Perhaps, if you doubt this, think about the opposite. If you want to feel bad, what do you need to do? Think bad thoughts. That's right. Think about all the times you screwed up or think of all the reasons to hate someone or feel angry about something. That's it, you know the drill!

There are two key steps involved in your thinking...

1. FOCUS (What you focus on)

And....

2. SELF TALK (What you say to yourself about it)

If you regularly put your attention on things of a highly negative nature, then naturally, you will feel upset and down. If you bring your attention to things of a more positive nature, you will feel more positive. Now you might already be thinking, James, why are you telling me this? Do you assume I have no brain and this; think bad feel bad, think good feel good thing, is news to me?! No, I'm quite sure you get this, at an intellectual level, but not yet at a full embodied level of understanding and that is what I want to impart to you here. So keep reading now, because I believe this understanding is absolutely central to having the experience of life you want.

When you think bad thoughts of other people, you own those thoughts. Only YOU hold and respond to your thoughts. That person could be off playing beach volleyball and yet a part of you is convinced that, if you just think enough bad thoughts about them, that ought to punish them! You can curse another person, you can get as angry as you want, but there's only one person who is feeling anything about this. Who? You of course! You. It's you and only you who is soaking up all the negative feeling of such thoughts. The other person gets nothing of it. Why? Because they're off responding to their own thoughts. THEIR thoughts, not YOURS. If you want a good life (and you do) then you really need to get good at generating the thoughts that you want to FEEL! Because YOU FEEL YOUR THOUGHTS, period. That's how it is.

Now am I saying always be happy and positive and pretend everything is fine even when it isn't? Am I saying let people walk all over you and never get angry or defend yourself? I'm not saying that at all. What I am saying is, endeavour, from now, to cut down on the stress and strain you put on yourself from any excessive negative focuses and self-talk. An incident may last one minute, but the focus on it and the self-talk around it could last days or even years. It's not what happens to us, but what we force ourselves to carry with us, that wears at us and erodes our sense of well-being. Stand up for yourself by all means, tell people when they are out of line and even take appropriate action, but then take charge of your focus and self-talk. Give your brain good things to focus on. This way you free up your internal life to carry far less with you and automatically generate the feelings you want to feel.

"Thoughts are the shadows of our feelings"

Friedrich Nietzsch

Yes, I know sometimes other people are crazy, annoying, stupid, selfish, harsh and even downright nasty perhaps. Yes, I know life can be horrendously unfair and harsh and tough and challenging. But this is why you need to get this bit right in your life. Life is tough enough as it is without being on your own back whipping yourself. You may say, "I'm not whipping me…I'm whipping them". No, you ARE whipping yourself because you're doing this in YOUR head. Holding resentment in yourself is one of the most self-destructive things you can do. With anger for others or yourself or anger at situations, you treat yourself as an emotional punch bag. If you've been doing this, even slightly, it's time to change all that and release yourself to a better experience of life.

So what's the answer? Start to become aware of what you are regularly putting your focus on and what you are saying to yourself. Take charge of your focus and your self-talk and place them onto more positive things. Realise, moaning and complaining and negative topics tend to be really boring anyway, especially when repeated over and over. When someone wrongs you, forgive them and if you can't; pity them. Depersonalise it; it's probably not much about you anyway. Refuse to change your emotional state for the negative attitude of another. See them as a misled child and you as the adult. Refuse to give bad thoughts space and time in your precious mind. Start to become more conscious and train yourself to be looking for positive things to focus on. Acknowledge the bad but refuse to focus deeply into negative topics. If you are around others who feel they have to talk about negatives too much then change the subject or get distance from them.

Start to point your mind at better things to think about. If you can't think of any, then your job is to gain new interests or new levels of interest in things you already do. Think and talk about them or about things you could create or accomplish. Think more about positive possibilities. Think about more positive things more often and you will become a more positive person. You will attract more positive people towards you, leading to new opportunities and positive circumstances. Practice gratitude and give thanks or blessings to people and things around you. Bless the food you eat, the bed you sleep in and even the ground you walk on if you wish. Quite frankly, anything of a positive nature to add some positive credits into the bank of your mind. As the saying goes:

"What you focus on EXPANDS in your reality"

Keep adding these positive thoughts consistently through whatever means you find and soon your mind will take over like on auto-pilot. You will feel a new sense of hope or opportunity and a surge of positive energy. You will notice more that's good around you.

Your self-esteem will rise and you will feel like you're gaining positive momentum in your life.

Another saying is:

"Where focus goes...energy flows."

Whatever you focus your attention on, especially with emotion involved, you energise the thoughts around it. Your brain is becoming trained to allow you to access those same thoughts and feelings again more easily. And so, again the message is to choose what you focus on and put emotional energy into. Energise the thoughts and things that you want your brain to keep reminding you of. If you get this right, you will energise the things that help you feel good and be automatically triggered back into positive thoughts and feelings more of the time.

Change the Meanings...Change the Feelings

Another key thing to be aware of is that behind most, if not all strong feelings, you will have likely created some MEANINGS. And it's these meanings that act like a code set up ready to trigger your feelings. It has been said that we humans are 'Meaning Making Mechanisms'. We make up what things mean to us. In turn we take these meanings and respond to them. It's like a needed attachment in order for us to feel something strongly. We might be quite calm about something until we create a negative meaning about it and attach it to ourselves. We may create the meaning that something means; "they don't respect me" and then feel angry about it. But until we created this negative meaning, we really had little emotion about it.

It's problematic when we make up negative meanings as interpretations of events. A person might tell themselves that the thing that happened MEANS they are a lost cause or that they will never have another chance, or something MEANS they are unloved or even unlovable and no-one accepts them for who they are. If you have been experiencing too many negative emotions recently, stop and ask yourself; what meanings have I been creating in my mind, that have been making me feel this way? Stop and write them down and as you look at them, start picking them apart. Question them, by asking yourself:

What else could this have really meant?

Why is this meaning just simply not true?

What is even silly or ridiculous about that meaning?

How am I going to think about this instead now?

In the field of Psychology this technique is known as 'Reframing' and it's powerful because, as mentioned, meanings work like a loaded code behind the scenes. Trigger that code and you trigger feelings. Imagine standing on a stage and hearing people applaud you after you just gave a performance. If you had never learned what applause was, in other words what it MEANT, then you would stand there confused. But knowing that applause MEANS you did well and MEANS people are showing their appreciation for you; you FEEL good.

A Quick Reframing Exercise for You

Let's demonstrate what you can do to get your conscious mind involved and start unpicking the negative meanings that your unconscious mind has been making.

Question:

What presently has been bothering you? Have you been experiencing stress or other negative emotions? Jot down the things that seem to have given you these feelings.

....
....
....
....
....
....
....
....
....

Now, looking at this, write out what MEANINGS you SUSPECT you may have been telling yourself:

....
....
....
....
....
....
....
....

....
....
....

Now look at these meanings and start to challenge them. Ask yourself: how is that an exaggeration? What else could this really mean? How is that meaning silly or ridiculous? What does this really mean instead?

You see, if you let unconscious mechanisms form all the meanings that are running in the background of your life, then how likely are you to have the FEELINGS you want? Sometimes stand back from your auto-mode in life and go: "Hang on....hang on....wow....now what's happening here? What am I telling myself about this? What negative or even plain false MEANINGS am I creating here? BECOME CONSCIOUS. Ask yourself; for me to be FEELING this way about this, what is it that I am telling myself? Come on brain…..what meanings? Then, like we just did, put those meanings on the chopping board and hack like crazy!

Step Into The Consciously Driven Life

If you allow your unconscious mind to run your life without any good conscious direction, you will likely survive well, but not have a great experience of life. Why do I say this? Because your unconscious mind is really all about protection and safety and much less about fulfilment and happiness. Remember your ancestors. They were survivors and had to have this primed awareness of anything that could be a threat.

In modern life we are far better set for survival with the establishment of societies and even medical advancements. However, we are still primed for fight or flight responses at a moment's notice. Someone cuts in front of us on the motorway and we react with rage. Someone says something to us and we make a negatively charged meaning of it far beyond what they ever intended. We stress ourselves and run through our mind numerous creative hallucinations of things which never actually happened. We feed them into the unconscious mechanism nevertheless and respond to things as if those hallucinations were real. We operate with a far too sensitised self-protection mechanism for the modern world.

So what's the answer. As far as I can tell, the answer is to get your conscious mind involved. Reveal to yourself what underlying errors your unconscious mind has made. Revealing a negative meaning, like you just did, can be like realising you've been walking around with a stone in your shoe. No wonder you were feeling bad. Asking questions to reveal these unhelpful meanings is like stopping, taking off your shoe and tipping the stone out. Ahhh, that's better! I ask you; how many stones are you walking around with? How many unnecessarily negative meanings have you auto-created, which you are going along with as if they are true? If you are walking through life with more negative feelings than positive ones, you've got stones in your shoes!

So again, what's the answer? Become more conscious; use your conscious mind to intervene. This is like a manager overseeing a project or a referee controlling a football match. Without a referee, a football match could become chaotic pretty quickly, with fouls and cheating and disorder prevailing. Likewise, if you leave that unconscious sucker up to its own devices, your emotional experience of life will likely be turbulent! Step in with your conscious mind regularly. Ask yourself questions like: what must I be telling myself in order for me to be feeling this way? What unhelpful meanings have I made? Coach yourself with your conscious mind. By doing so, you uproot weeds that have been festering and replant flowers in their place.

A Summary

Ultimately, your life is about feelings. Your choices and behaviours are driven by what's behind them and what's behind them is an endless desire for the feelings you want. The human mind is a 'Meaning Making Mechanism' and it's really when something 'means' something to you, that you 'feel' something. If something doesn't mean anything to you, you don't feel anything for it. And so, by using your ability to consciously intervene, you can coach yourself to ensure that you are filtering out potentially damaging meanings and replace them with ones which have you feel better.

Start putting your attention on positive things more often. If another person wrongs you in any way, do what you can to de-personalise it. In other words, get yourself to realise, it's really not so much about you anyway. Take charge of your self-talk. Refuse to have your mind pointed at negative things too long. This doesn't mean you live with your head in the clouds. Acknowledge the bad, just don't have your mind live there. Remember, in order to have the feelings you want in life, you must generate the thoughts that support them. It really is up to you.

"The mind is its own place, and in itself, can make a Heaven of Hell, a Hell of Heaven"

John Milton, Paradise Lost

PART 3
Now...
What To Do?

If you have done yourself the justice of engaging with the first two parts of this book, then you will now be clearer on who you are and what you want. But for now, let's shift our focus towards the question of what you are going to do. What are you going to spend your life mainly doing from this point forwards? What is it, for you, that is worth your time? What could you throw your heart into, enjoy doing and get really good at? What might also hold some great service and value to the world around you? What pursuits are worthy of YOU?

Now that you know your core values, have at least an idea of your life's purpose and understand what motivates you, start to think about what fits YOU best. Use your self-knowledge to empower yourself. Stay with things that align with your values, meet your needs, suit your personality and help fulfil your purpose. I think you'll agree, this way you're far more likely to flourish and bring good things to your own life and others.

Part 3 is going to take you further now and help you gain some key understandings that support you in having the courage and inspiration to turn your ideas into action.

Create Value

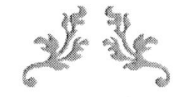

> "Strive not to be a success, but rather to be of value"

Albert Einstein

What you want to do is initially going to fall into one of the following three things.

You're either going to:

1) Get really good at something

2) Find the right team…or

3) Create something

Ultimately, in time, it's more likely that you will do a combination of at least two of these, perhaps all three.

Get Really Good at ONE Thing

If you commit yourself to something and gain specialised knowledge or skill in an in-demand area, no doubt in time, if you go for it, you will be in demand. Do it well enough and you'll make a living; master it and you'll make a killing! Traditional schooling does not help us to garner the right mentality for focusing in on one thing. If you got an A in one subject but D's in all others, you might be branded a failure. But this isn't how life works at all.

Fortunately, especially from now, in this modern, super-connected world that you live in, you really only have to be good at one thing. Why? Because if you take care of that one aspect for others and serve the value that it offers them, then other people can cover all the other areas for you. If you just stop and think about it for a moment, you might realise; it's a really beautiful thing. Our lives are about TEAMWORK, whether you've been fully aware of it or not.

Here's the deal: You do your thing well and collect money for it in exchange for the value you offer. With that money you can tap into the endless ocean of value that other people can offer you. Look around you right now. What things do you see that others have created for you, which have great value to you? Perhaps your home with all of its contents, functions and appliances. The shelter it proves you, the warmth and running water, just to mention a few. Food, sown and grown and stocked and transported to you, by no effort of your own. The immense value of endless thousands of other people's skills and dedications at your beck and call. All thanks to our great, intricate network of connection, of which you are part. And here's the great deal; you do what you do best and let the rest of us take care of everything else.

So, what might be your one thing? One thing that, if you truly dedicated yourself to it, you really could have great value with it to other people? Think of a sports person who might not be good at writing or maths or giving speeches and yet they excel at their sport. They have a narrow band of skillsets honed on their craft. But do they really need to be great at other things, when they are the best at what they do? Think of the singer with the wonderful voice. Do they need to be the best at 10 other things?

Think even of a brand that impacts the marketplace. The ones that make a big impact are nearly always ones that initially specialise in a single specific product or service. They master that one thing first before they think about diversifying. Apple Inc started with their own type of computer and didn't diversify to other products until they dominated a market share.

Amazon, at one time, was really only known for ONE product. Can you remember what? That's right; books. Founder Jeff Bezos, now the richest man in the world, ensured that his company would make the biggest splash possible in ONE pond. Amazon gained international recognition as the 'go to' place to buy any book in the world. It's only after they built their foundations in books that they had the ability to spread out successfully into so many other things.

Think of a laser. How is it that it can cut through steel? By concentrating all of its power in a narrow beam of focus. If it disperses its energy too wide, it never breaks through. In the same way, think about what it is that you would like to focus in on. If you are at the age now where you have left school and you're seeking employment or thinking of creating something of your own, consider how you might narrow your focus. How might you now harness your interest or passion and focus on a specific beam of value?

What's YOUR Nectar?

In a colony of Bees there are different types of Bees with different jobs. There's the 'Queen Bee' who lays all the eggs, 'Worker Bees' who maintain the hive and what have been named 'Drone Bees' who fertilise the

Queen. The Worker Bees have various job roles at different stages of life; nursing, cleaning and foraging for nectar. They don't fret about their roles it seems, because they instinctively know that by working in harmony, they create something far more magnificent for them all. Different roles but perfect synergy; each Bee having value to the whole and happily so.

What kind of Bee are you? We humans are like Bees, only our colonies and far more complex with many more types of Bee. Some humans are the worker Bees who like to design or build or expand or maintain. Others are the inventor Bees who create and think up solutions. Then there are service Bees who support the structure of already established colonies and hives. Then entertainer Bees who help us relax and feel good and many, many more types. Keep thinking; what sort of Bee can you best Beee! Somehow, we all fit together. Perhaps by tuning up your awareness for the value of what's around you and your appreciation for the service of others, you can start to better notice what value YOU can offer.

Climbing One Mountain…To The TOP!!

Let me finish this point by offering a metaphor for your life. If you were climbing in a magnificent mountain range, would you prefer to climb half way up 5 mountains or to the top of one? Which would give you the better view? By climbing to the top of one mountain, you get to see the view. From there you gain new perspectives. Not only have you gained skill and self-belief, but you can then survey the horizon better. From the summit of one, you see the landscape unfold around you. You can see what valleys and paths lead where and if there are other mountains you want to conquer, you can start to plan the best routes.

Finding Your Team

Finding the right team means giving your services and commitment to an organisation or company and this might suit you best. Alternatively, if you're highly creative and self-driven, you may seek to bring together your own team to help you manifest of your own ideas. Whatever you choose, the extent of your success will always be down to one overarching thing…

How much <u>VALUE</u> can you give or create?

You will always be rewarded to the degree that you offer value. If you want to get paid well by a company, you have to become valuable to that company. If you want to create something and make a lot of money from it, you have to create and serve a lot of value. Every financial transaction is one of value. You are happy to hand over £10 of your money for something that you want more than that £10. In your perception, that thing, to you, is worth more than the £10. If not, you would choose not to get it.

Start thinking about how you can be of highest value to the world around you? What interests, talents or skills do you have that you sense you could have value to others with? Ideally interests where you have a natural alignment of your strengths? What are you already good at, that if you were to go 'all in' and commit yourself to it, you could be really good at? Alternatively, what are you passionate about, which could align well with the mission and values of an organisation? Is there something that you already know you care strongly about where, if you were to only align yourself with the right team, you could make a difference?

Recognising Value

Now a person might think about someone like a sports star getting paid great sums of money and wonder what value they contribute and yet they do. If someone is outstanding at something, people want to see them and will be willing to pay a ticket price. So you can even see here how value is still the central factor. What about a musician? Same thing. People don't want to listen to music they don't like, but creating music that people like IS creating value. Think of a waiter or waitress giving a good service. A person will tip based on the value they feel they received. There are all sorts of value transactions across our world every day. Some may make far less sense to you than others, but remember people pay for what THEY PERCEIVE IS VALUE. If a person feels good feelings from something, they perceive to gain value from it and, perhaps, rightly so.

To get yourself thinking creatively about your options, I suggest you make a list of ways that different people share value. If you are focusing on your career then make this list all about how people make money doing all sorts of different things. Stretch your mind and even think of some obscure jobs or trades or things people do that nevertheless pay them financially in return. Remember, it's not always actual value or value agreed on by all people, but an individual's perception of value that they respond to. One person may be willing to pay a far higher price for something that they perceive to be of great value to them than others. Auction houses and even property deals are based on what someone is willing to pay. So go ahead and make your own list of ways in which people create or share value. Do this to establish a wider awareness in your mind of value transactions and allow your mind to percolate ideas for what you might ultimately choose.

No Short-Cuts!

The creating and giving of value could be thought of as akin to an irrefutable Law of life. It is here to stay. Try to short-cut this at your own peril. Some may gain financial success by scamming others, deceiving, stealing, but they will never be celebrated people, always wretched. Even those who don't get imprisoned are missing the understanding that they are really bankrupting their soles; trading off the fulfilment of their values and robbing their heart of ever really feeling good about themselves. Perhaps some do it from desperation and others because they simply fail to recognise the value that they could have. Sad as it is, do not fret over these people, even if once in a while they get you. Pity them for a moment and then get back to creating value. Nothing gives more back to you than knowing that you are of great value to others and the world around you.

In Essence...

Is it time for you to understand your value to the world? Do you sense yet what value you might bring to offer? Will you create something of your own or join forces with a team or perhaps many teams over time? Will you dedicate yourself to a craft, a skill or subject and dare to commit to the best you can be? I say, take some time to think about value and what you want to do; it's a big enough world to give you options. So, perhaps it's time for you to get creative and enjoy the process of exploring what you can do.

"Help enough other people get what they want, and you'll never have any trouble getting what you want"

Anthony Robbins

The Risk of Not Risking

"If you are not willing to risk the unusual, you will have to settle for the ordinary"

Jim Rohn

Many people avoid the risk of doing something they would really like to do, all the while taking the greatest risk of all; that of living unfulfilled and dying empty. I think many of us fear the wrong things. We assume that by taking a 'safe path' things will work out. But there's always a price to pay, isn't there?

Much can be learned about risk from playing sports. Personally, I'm a great tennis fan and have learned that if you try to play safe; you lose! It's not safe at all. In tennis we have a saying that goes:

"Are you playing to win….or are you playing not to lose?"

They are two very different approaches with a very different energy behind them.

Think about your own choices in life. Have you been playing to win or have you been playing to not lose? In reality, is there ever really no risk in anything? Is playing it safe actually safe? Isn't the truth really that risk is a part of life and one that you must embrace or risk far more? If you're not willing to risk in the name of things you care for, then life will hand you other risks regardless. The risk of wasting your life in pursuits with no meaning for you. The risk of spending precious time with people who don't support you in becoming your best. The risk of being with people who subconsciously prey on you, because they see your self-doubt and feel that knowing you makes them feel better about their own insecurities. The risk denying your natural alignment for life; your talents, gifts or desires. The risk of looking back with regret.

Run and Keep Running

As mentioned earlier, in 2002 I went travelling for some time. And, although I didn't 'find myself' (because I didn't have this book!), I did take some chances to step outside my comfort zone and stretch myself. One of these experiences involved Hang Gliding. You know; the one where you basically run off the edge of a cliff holding what looks from a distance like a giant paper aero plane above you. I did it tandem with an instructor of course. Alone would have been a poor judgement of risk! My instructor made it very clear to me; "We run, and we keep running until we are clear of the cliff edge, ok?" Just in case I hadn't quite got it, he laid out the consequences, saying "If you do not keep running until the edge and try to slow down near the edge, we will fall down the cliff and die. Do you understand?". I got it! Scarred as I was to run, I was far more afraid now not to. I ran and kept running until my legs were flapping in the air beneath me. Talk about a leap of faith! It was a thrill and one which I won't forget.

The thing about playing 'not to lose' is that it automatically focuses you on the wrong thing; 'losing'. It forces your mind to spark doubt inducing thoughts of things going wrong. When you tell a child "not to spill that milk" or "not to play ball games in the sitting room", what do they do? It still amazes me to hear adults shout bad ideas at children and then act so surprised when the child does that very thing. The adult expects the feeble word "not" to delete the glaring image that THEY PUT into the child's mind a moment ago. "I told you not to PLAY WITH THOSE MATCHES IN THE BARN!" The brain moves towards the dominant thought in any moment, perhaps especially ones which offer rich imagery. When you play to win you give your mind clear instructions; see this, do that.

"Stop being afraid of what could go wrong, and start being excited about what could go right"

Anthony Robbins

Lean Into It

Going for something with full focus and intention reduces risk. If you hit a tennis ball too cautiously too often, you'll get beaten, at least by anyone who's any good. To win a tennis game you must apply a strategy of playing to win. Hit that ball and hit it with the intention to direct it and win. You have to risk losing to risk winning. A bad driver might think that it's best to join a fast motorway at a speed of just 30 miles per hour. You know, "just to be safe!" Sometimes tiptoeing in is the greatest risk because you fail to commit yourself in ways that have you reveal to yourself what you are actually capable of. The dabbler in any endeavour, never makes acquaintance with their potential and only gets to judge things from a distorted perspective. It's only when you fully go into something and commit to it, that you lower the risk increasingly more as you gain the knowledge and skills required to make the thing a success.

What risks have you been avoiding while ignoring the very risk of doing so? We are of course only talking about perceived risks, not threats to life. Perceived risks of taking action on a good idea or introducing yourself to someone new at the 'risk' of them not being polite to you. Remind yourself, when you risk...you grow...you learn. The very act of stepping up towards that which you fear, gives you the chance to be the person you want to be.

Read that again…

The very act of stepping up towards that which you fear, gives you the chance to be the person you want to be.

Beware of Unworthy Risks

Having offered these thoughts, I feel I must balance them with some cautions. In this modern and fast changing world of ours, we must judge what is a fair risk and use our intelligence. Remember in chapter five I suggested the 'Best, Worst, Likely Case Scenarios' method for making decisions and this might apply well to anything that might seem like a risk. If, when you ask yourself what the worst-case outcome might be, dozens of concerns fill your mind and only one thing comes to mind when you ask yourself about the best case scenario, then you may be better off not taking action on that thing. This chapter is about stepping into what you really want in life, not falling prey to schemes and scams or making poor judgements.

In the previous chapter on creating value, I raised a caution 'not to take short cuts'. It holds true not only in avoiding the temptation to cheat people out of value, but also in avoiding getting cheated yourself. Your intention might be good, but if your commitment isn't, you might be tempted at times to think that someone else can do it all for you. If you'll only join their scheme and pay all of your savings into it, then their brilliance will do your success for you! Such thoughts are likely to be unworthy risks. Realise, you must take it on yourself to develop your value and this will take dedication and effort over time. You do this through choosing your path and building the knowledge and skills that increase your value to others. Others can help you, but never risk assuming someone else will do it for you.

"It's your road and yours alone.
Others may walk it with you, but
no-one can walk it for you"

Rumi

A Final Thought...

Perhaps it's a shame that we don't have more things like Hang Gliding that disallows us from cowering from risk, where our perceived pain of not committing to it is greater than that of just going for it! Perhaps the greatest risk is to never risk anything. If you don't risk anything, by default you risk everything, missing out on life. Life IS risk. What if your mother hadn't risked having you?! What if your brave ancestors hadn't risked venturing further afield? You'd perhaps be sitting in a cave right now without any of the things around you that make your life better.

Live with awareness of real risks, but also with that of illusions that would steal you away from your better self. Now that you know your values and have clarity about who you are and what you want, you're prepared to identify those things which align with you well. I think you'd agree, it's far riskier to go through life without this self-knowledge. And so, to make decisions that serve your purpose and life's needs and values, what risk is that? May your clarity and wisdom guide you in.

"A ship is safe in harbour, but that is not what a ship was built for"

William H. Shedd

Lean Into Failure

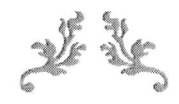

> "Sometimes it takes a wrong turn to get you to the right place"

Mandy Hale

When you were a baby and then a toddler, you went through phases from barely moving, to crawling, to standing, to walking. You had to learn all the large and small distinctions needed to feel and adjust, to balance and finally walk. Fortunately, you were instinctively curious and determined. You had an unstoppable strategy. A willingness to make whatever number of attempts were required, over whatever time was required. No wonder you can walk! You had both the willingness and ability to fall on your bottom over and over and over again without ever feeling deterred or defeated. You kept trying again and again until you got it.

You see, this was before you learned the human concept of failure. Your mind back then was perfectly pure and un-interfered with and so you simply paid attention to the feedback that would guide you to inevitable success. You had a magnificent mindset, one of complete openness. One which embraced all feedback, making no negative, interfering judgements. One which was purely curious to explore and discover what works and what doesn't. Not taking anything personally or wasting time creating unhelpful meanings. A mindset of being curious and happy to make endless adjustments UNTIL you had the outcome wanted.

What could you accomplish in your life if you were to return to that mindset? It's an interesting thought is it not? What could you get really good at if you were to drop all concern about failing and return to your innate willingness to take all feedback not as failure, but as learning?

So, What Happened?

At one point in your early development, you started to learn from other people that you are supposed to "get things right". You learned that it was bad to get things wrong, it's all about being right, answering correctly. If you put your hand up to answer a question, you might be humiliated and told off if you answer wrongly. You only look good, sound good, get rewarded IF you get things right. So, get things right…..get things right. If you make a mistake, quickly cover it up and pretend you got it right….get it right…get it right.

Can you see the interference coming in? This compulsive way of perceiving things supported by early authority figures creates conditioned layers of belief about the way things are and the way YOU MUST BE. The adult version of this still looks for approval and recognition of their rightness. They hate to fail and so they hate to take any risks or move outside of their comfort zone. They hate to be wrong and will not be told that they are wrong. They check their facts regularly in case anyone was to quiz them, and they look forward to moments where they can share their knowledge, whether others are interested or not, because it proves that THEY ARE RIGHT!

There's a great saying to keep in mind and it goes like this: "Do you want to be right, or do you want to be effective?" Think about this when you have a difference of opinion with someone.

Embrace Failure Again

Perhaps it's no coincidence that 'failure' is the name given to lifting a weight until you can't do any more repetitions. If you want to strengthen your muscles, then you must "push to failure". Being often in that 'failure zone' where it's hard for you to lift, is the shortest route to muscle growth and therefore success. This exertion forces the muscle to grow. This 'failure' is the only way to get stronger muscles. Body builders and athletes know that this leads them to strength and greater performance.

I say this: get back to your innate pure ability to be wrong or right or anything at all. Be willing to fail. Be willing to fail a thousand times if needed. Failure is the only true route to success. If you really want to succeed, then fail big, fail fast, fail repeatedly. Keep learning from each failure. Accumulate and absorb those lessons and over time, you will be so knowledgeable and good in your chosen endeavours, that others will only stand and wonder how you do it. Remember; good decisions come from experience and experience comes from making bad decisions. The great Mark Twain said that and how right he was. Make decisions and take action with your best present knowledge. If you win you win and if you don't; well then you learn in such ways that you can win in future.

"I have learnt more from my failures than my successes"

Sir Richard Branson

Trying to succeed in any worthwhile endeavour without having any failure on the way, is like trying to cross a field without getting any mud on your shoes. If you keep only looking for the safe, dry patches, you'll never get across. If you're taking something on you must be willing to get your feet dirty. In the film Rocky Balboa, Rocky imparts to his son "It ain't about how hard you can hit, it's about how hard you can get hit and keep moving forwards. That's how winning is done. You've got to be willing to take the hits." Life can feel like panning for gold sometimes. Life only really opens up to those who are willing to sift through the dirt and rubble and keep going regardless. When you have a purpose in mind, something of meaning to you, you will happily keep sifting until your gold is found.

There Is No Failure Only Feedback

One modern branch of Psychology, which you might have heard of, is NLP (Neuro Linguistic Programming). The founders: Richard Bandler and John Grinder, laid down a key principle for applying any of their techniques…

"There is no failure, only feedback"

The most effective approach to most things is to apply a solution and then notice whether it's working. If it is, then do more of the same and if it isn't, then apply something else. Keep observing the result and adjusting the approach UNTIL you get the outcome you are after. There is no such thing as failure if you only keep going with a flexible approach. When you were learning to walk, you didn't come to a point where you stopped and considered never trying again. You didn't say to yourself; "What will other people think of me falling over like this? It's embarrassing. I must be stupid. Right, that's it, I'll just have to make do with crawling for this lifetime." You didn't think like that at all because you hadn't been poisoned with that way of thinking yet. No, at that stage of life, you were YOU. You were who you are now, but without the interference. And the more you can purify your mind once more and remove the nonsense, the more you will take on things with joy and flair, stepping into the experiences of life, learning, absorbing and growing.

The Power of Persistence

It was early summer 2001 and I had volunteered to do a job tidying up after the Queen's Club Tennis Tournament; the posh grass court tennis tournament in England leading up to Wimbledon. As I was meandering around the sides of courts looking for something to clean, I noticed Goran Ivanisevic was on one of the courts practicing his famously fast serve. Ivanisevic had already been in three Wimbledon finals at that stage and lost them all. He was perhaps the best server of the game and as I watched on from a privileged close position, he kept serving and serving and serving. I went off for lunch and when I came back, he was still there, serving. I went off again and even some hours later he was still there, serving and serving. That year Goran Ivanisevic beat Pat Rafter in the final and finally succeeded in winning Wimbledon. Goran's endless hours of dedicated practice paid off.

Fisherman, Fireman and Farmers all know of the power of persistence. The fisherman must be patient as part of their persistent plan. They must be willing to wait or move and get up and go when the going is good. A fireman must be persistent not only in progressing through a burning building, but in finding alternative ways in. A farmer must keep sowing, watering and harvesting, often all day long and all night too if that's what's required. There's little time to fret over failed actions, persistence corrects all and drives home the results.

Use The Law of Large Numbers

In order for you to attain all that you want in life, life will likely require you to conduct a large numbers campaign. More likely in fact many large numbers campaigns across the range of endeavours you take on. Author of 'The Law of Large Numbers', Dr Gary Goodman, claims that you can virtually make your success in life inevitable. That is, if only you are willing to stay long enough with any endeavour and take enough of the relevant actions that lead you there.

The golfer who hits the most balls, the runner who runs the most miles, the actor who stays behind to rehearse again one more time, the businessperson who starts early and stays late, the salesperson who knocks on the most doors. If you will only put the numbers in, then in time, you will get the numbers out, including the ones in your bank account. Ultimately, you will be rewarded for your persistence. If you are willing to fail and fail again and yet not see it as failure, but as feedback then; just as you successfully learned to walk, you will succeed at other things.

As Winston Churchill said:

"Success is going from failure to failure without losing enthusiasm"

Have you heard the story of America's most prolific inventor, Thomas A. Edison? The man who invented the electric light bulb and had a record of 1093 patents for his mass of inventions. Edison was well known for making huge numbers of attempts at his inventions. He would keep going until he broke through. So the story goes; when interviewed once by the press, a reporter asked him:

"Mr Edison, you have tried and failed to create an electric light bulb several thousand times now. Sir, why do you persist? Surely it is clear that we are destined to operate by night with paraffin lantern or by candlelight."

Edison is recorded to have replied something along the following lines:

"My dear man, you simply do not understand the way the world works. I have not failed thousands of times, I have succeeded thousands of times in eliminating the ways the electric light bulb doesn't work. Each attempt rewards me with new awareness which I will use to create the light bulb that does work".

You see, Edison knew things. He didn't think of failure like most people have been conditioned to and certainly used a large numbers philosophy and the quality of persistence. Just stop for a moment now, look around you and acknowledge; what would you not have right now, if there was no electric lighting!

Quantity or Quality?

So, what of the quantity vs quality argument? Some people may say it's all very well doing a high quantity of something, but if it isn't good quality then what's the point? What are your thoughts on this?

Personally, I somewhat agree with this and if ever you match together a high quantity with high quality, then, I think we'd all agree, you'll do very well. Look at Apple Inc. whose products are known for their quality and sell in huge quantity too. Little wonder Apple is one of the world's most successful companies.

However, let me offer you a different tangent to thinking about this too. Often a high quality of something is reached only through a high quantity. In order for you to get really good at something, you may have to practice it over and over again. At first your quality may be poor and that can't be helped. It's only through the repetition and rehearsal of the skills that you finally get to the quality level you've been aiming at. If you are reading for a degree or doctorate, but you are only putting in a few hours a week of study for it, then you might not be putting in the quantity of time needed to get the grade. Often quality comes from an initial large quantity of efforts and until you have put in the time and repetitions, you simply can't create the quality because you haven't had the chance to get the feel or learn the key distinctions that only reveal themselves with time and practice. In reality, we always fail until we succeed, it's part of the learning process of anything. So we might as well get on and fail faster. I sometimes think of success as a deeply wrapped present, wrapped in layers of failure. You don't get to receive the present if you are unwilling to unwrap it. Start now and get ripping!

Before I conclude this chapter, let me make one key distinction. None of what's said here means that you should persist with a wrong strategy. Persistence should be used with the willingness to test and realign your efforts, not to keep going with an obviously flawed plan. What's that saying…

"Insanity is doing the same thing over and over and expecting a different result".

Think of Edison. The real quality for you to garner is to be willing to lean into failure, so you can use that feedback to adapt. Left a bit, right a bit, change this out and bring this in. Keep flexible and changing your approach until you find your way.

Go Forth And Multiply!

Now, with your self-knowledge and understandings and the quality of, call it; 'flexible persistence', you can become an unstoppable force. Hopefully, for all our sakes, a force for good! Be prepared to throw out some of what you've picked up and get back to your pure magnificent self. The one willing to fall on your arse and get back up. Be prepared also to make a large number of efforts in any endeavour you engage in. But I do have one respectful request of you: Be prolific by all means, but not wasteful. Don't junk people or the environment around you. Persist in ways that are good for all.

FINALLY THINK!

What ONE thing, if you were to only increase the number of times you do it, would have the greatest positive impact on your life?

"Nothing in this world can take the place of persistence. Talent will not; nothing is more common than unsuccessful people with talent. Genius will not; unrewarded genius is almost a proverb. Education will not; the world is full of educated derelicts. PERSISTENCE and DETERMINATION alone are OMNIPOTENT"

Calvin Coolidge

Take Responsibility

"Accept responsibility for your life. Know that it is you who will get you where you want to go, no one else"

Les Brown

Taking responsibility for yourself; your actions, your behaviours and your results, is a self-empowering thing. Shirking responsibility and looking to blame others instead, is a self-disempowering thing. Taking responsibility really means stepping into your mature freedom. It's like a positive agreement with yourself which says, I permit me to go for things, explore and expand myself. If I make mistakes, I'm ok with that because I learn, I grow, I adapt. The alternative of blaming, moaning and complaining is like handing your power away. It subliminally suggests that you are more like a powerless victim, rather than anyone capable of good things.

The reason why we need to remind ourselves of our responsibility, is because our childhood may have been rife with the propensity to blame. "It wasn't me Sir". "He started it Miss". As children we perceived taking responsibility as being punished and so in our brains, we linked pain to it. I doubt anyone is going to take a slipper to your bottom these days! In fact, really the far opposite is true where, if you are noticed as someone who can step up and take responsibility, then others will probably reward you.

Taking responsibility for yourself and all that you do, allows you to learn. Reflect on the last chapter about failure as feedback. It's the person who sees failure as a terminal thing rather than a learning opportunity, who tries to shirk responsibility. The person who takes responsibility has the mental openness to look for the gifts from that previous experience. Perhaps like a great detective, who stays calm and objective to the situation. They can take the lessons and make progress, not despite the failures, but because of them.

A Definition

If we break down the word responsibility, what we get is RESPONSE-ABILITY. The ability to respond. Isn't this what you want? The ability to respond and adapt to outcomes as they unfold so that you can keep adjusting your approach until you find the best ways. So, think of this once more; you are response…ABLE.

Motivational speaker Zig Ziglar said…

"It's not your aptitude, but your attitude that will determine your altitude"

You can never really get ahead of a bad attitude. Embracing responsibility is core to a good attitude.

Boosting Your Self-Image

One of my favourite books is a powerful little book called Psycho-Cybernetics by Maxwell Maltz. I know it's a strange title perhaps, but it's full of great information. The dominant point is that, as a human, you are held back or driven on by the way you see yourself; your 'self-image'. This is central to how well you will do in any endeavour.

If you have a poor self-image, that will lower your confidence and self-belief and interfere with what you do. Taking full responsibility for yourself is one of the core things that you can do to enhance and strengthen your self-image. Again, think of what you are subliminally communicating to yourself when you are happy to take responsibility. You send positive signals resounding in yourself saying: I'm in charge of me and my life. I can lean into projects with confidence, because I know I will be able to respond and take positive action when needed.

Denying responsibility from yourself, is denying a chance to build your self-image higher. If you choose to blame outside of yourself too much, you start to feel like you are at the effect of the world around you more than you are. Beware of victim mode! You are not a victim; you are in the driving seat of your life. Even if you were a victim of something when you were younger, you are now an adult and like a Lion or Lioness on the plains of the Savanna; you have all the strengths and qualities needed to take charge and make life what you want it to be.

Affirm It To Yourself

By affirming to yourself regularly that you take responsibility for your life, your decisions, your mistakes and your successes; you fully own your life and step up to the adult plain of life. Apparently, some species of birds literally push their young out of the nest. They go, "Go on.... you can fly now for yourself....bugger off!". We humans tend to be gentler than this and yet, taking responsibility for yourself is a huge gift. Inevitably you will see yourself BETTER. As more capable, more confident, more appealing and valuable to the world around you. What greater gift can you receive than the gift of these sorts of feelings about yourself?

Here is a short and yet powerful affirmation to help you increase your sense of taking responsibility and I accredit this to master speaker and one of my true heroes; 'Brain Tracy'.

"I am responsible"

It's so simple and yet so powerful. When you say this to yourself repeatedly, it has a tremendous effect inside you. Try it. Right now, pause from reading this and say to yourself "I am responsible". Saying it again and again with feeling; like you mean it. Then keep saying it another 10 or 20 times. Once done continue reading.

Now, how do you feel in this moment after saying that simple affirmation? Perhaps you feel quite good, quite positive or confident. I know I always feel a sense of empowerment and motivation after saying this. And what's the price? Perhaps one minute of your time. Brain Tracy is right, this simple, concise affirmation impacts you and how you see yourself. Take a moment to say it often and remind yourself "I am responsible". If you have a morning or evening ritual, add this affirmation into it.

In Summary

Earlier in the book, I mentioned Victor Frankle, the man who suffered the Nazi prison camps and wrote the book 'Man's Search for Meaning'. Frankle's central point is that your ability to choose your responses to things is the one thing that no-one can ever take from you, no matter what happens. The Nazi's killed his family, tortured and killed his friends, imprisoned him for years in wretched conditions, but the one thing he held onto was his ability to choose his response to what happened. They could take everything else from him, but they couldn't take that. He could still choose his response. So, embrace this; you have tremendous power to choose what you experience in life. Each decision can be like forging a bend in a river; with each choice you make in life, you are shaping your experience of life.

Remember responsibility isn't blame. It's not negative at all; it's highly positive. If you want to be a leader, then heed this strongly. Even if you don't see yourself as a leader, the fact is you are the leader of YOUR life. You might have sensed already in life; you have a whole world inside yourself that you need to lead. A person may feel motivated at times, but then Monday morning comes and they feel lazy. In order to be effective in life, you need to lead yourself. After all, if you're not responsible for you, then who is?

"The moment you take responsibility for everything in your life, is the moment you can change anything in your life"

Hal Elrod

Remain Flexible

"A tree that is unbending is easily broken"

Lao Tzu

Life is a River, not a Runway

One of Bruce Lee's most famous sayings was...

"Be like water".

He would say,

"Water always adapts to its circumstances. If I pour water into a cup, it becomes the cup, if I pour it into a teapot, it becomes the teapot. It's the softest thing in the world and yet it can penetrate rock!"

It's perhaps easy to think how this can apply in the context of fighting, where you need to constantly flow and adapt to what your opponent does. But this really also applies to life in a wider context.

Think of a river. How many times does it come up against an obstacle and yet find a way round it? It bends, it winds, it adapts. A river demonstrates the ultimate persistence. It adapts no set number of times, but infinitely until it reaches its destiny. It doesn't stop to complain about its obstacles, it immediately goes to work adapting. Imagine if you were to become more like this in life; how could this help you? After all, you already know there will be challenges on the way to any worthwhile endeavour.

Perhaps decide to embrace life just as it is right now. Accept events ahead of time. If someone crashes into your car, spending hours afterwards fretting and thinking angry thoughts is just wasted time. It doesn't allow you to go back in time and stop it happening. Anything that has happened has already happened. Even something three seconds ago is now gone, and you cannot go back and change that. So, don't fuss about what's occurred, take it as it is and move forward. Who knows, someone bumping into your car might even be an opportunity to meet someone interesting or learn something new.

Life is far more like a river than a straight section of road; you will need to adapt. Again, coming back to self-awareness of your purpose and values in particular, being clear about YOU helps you stay on track regardless of what happens. Your purpose and values are great guides for your life because there isn't just one way to fulfil them.

Dealing With Setbacks

Think of a young sports person who has immense potential. They train hard every day for years. They put everything they have into it. They dream and harness their hopes for the future, and they look like they might become 'the next big thing'. Then, one day, they suffer a terrible injury. One that only gets worse with the intensity of training required at that level. Now what?! They feel devastated, distraught, like their dream has been stolen from them before it even started. For some time, they fester in how cruel life can be, how harsh and unfair. What now? That was their dream; what now?

At times you might have to let go of some strategy or goal that isn't working. Does this mean giving up? Does this mean losing permanently? Think again of a river meeting hard rock. If a river has to meander and turn away from an area, it does so and finds another way on.

Think of that sports person again. They have, through their training and dedication, built within themselves winning qualities and skills, not just physically, but so much more. Qualities that they can use in other things. Sometimes you may need to return to your core and ask yourself what you're really trying to do. That person wanted to be a sports star and that may have been all that was in their awareness all those years. And yet, remember, that sport is really a PASSION of theirs, not a PURPOSE. If they can tap into an understanding behind it, perhaps they can re-ignite themselves into something equally fulfilling or maybe something even better! What's the real purpose of their life? They wanted to be a sports star, but in order to what? Yes, a sports star....so that what? Look behind the obvious and find the way forward.

"I wanted to be a sports star...

So that I can inspire people like I was inspired by this person when I was 6 years old. So that I can feel a sense of love from people like I felt for them. So, I can express myself and give value to others and encourage them."

Great, now find other ways to do that!

Looking from Higher Ground

You might have watched adventure movies, where our followed main character is lost somewhere, perhaps in a desert, jungle or forest. Usually, they go through a really hard time and due to their struggles, we sympathise and hope for them. There's almost always a moment where they struggle to believe they will ever find a way out and for a moment, they fall into despair.

Then suddenly, they see a way to higher ground and when they climb up; the way forward reveals itself to them once again. Coming back to your purpose is like your personal trek to higher ground. If your present approach doesn't seem to be working or you're stuck against obstacles, coming back to your Purpose will allow you to see from higher perspective. As you survey your options, you might realise what other routes you could take that still lead there.

Staying Flexible in Your Approach

There are many inspiring stories of people who came up against obstacle after obstacle but found a way through. One of my favourites is the story of Silvester Stallone. During his birth the physician used a pair of forceps to deliver him and accidentally severed a nerve in his face. This left him partially paralysed in his lip, tongue and chin. This didn't make it easy for young Silvester when auditioning for acting roles. He got rejection after rejection. By his late twenties things got so bad for him that his wife left him, and he even had to sell his dog on a street corner to have money for food. He decided to start writing scripts and it was this change of approach that somehow became his breakthrough. After writing the script for Rocky and sharing it with dozens of producers, finally one producer saw the potential. Stallone negotiated the lead role in his own creation and of course, the rest is history. As mentioned earlier, Stallone had decided that his purpose in life was "to inspire people". He wrote the script for Rocky after watching a boxing match between Mohammed Ali and a little known boxer who, against all odds, went the distance with Ali. This inspired something inside him and it transpired through him to write Rocky. Ultimately this allowed him to come right back to being an actor as he wanted, but via a different route.

Of course, we've all heard of McDonald's, who hasn't right? But do you know the story of how it started? It was 1955, a travelling salesman by the name of Ray Kroc, was frustrated by his lack of success. He was now 52 years old and had spent years trying to come up with great ideas to no avail. At this point he was selling milkshake machines to restaurants, when he came across the unique restaurant of the McDonald's brothers. He was astounded by how quickly the food was served. Right away he started thinking about what this little restaurant could become if he could only replicate it over and over again. It wasn't Kroc's own baby though, his own ideas had previously all failed. If Kroc hadn't stayed open-minded and flexible in his approach, he would never have ignited his vision for the brand that we all know.

Those are just two of my favourites, but there are many more stories of people who had to keep a persistent, flexible approach. What about that of the great

Scientist Albert Einstein? He didn't start speaking or reading till a later than average age. What about our friend Thomas Edison, the great inventor? Told by teachers that he was too stupid to learn anything and fired from jobs for being "unproductive"! Henry Ford, the great car manufacturer, failed in five other ventures before having his success. That great British Prime Minister: Winston Churchill, was placed in the lowest division in the lowest class at school. Later he twice failed the entrance exam to the Royal Military Academy at Sandhurst. Walt Disney had to keep adapting and changing his approach too. After being fired from an animation job for a newspaper for "lacking imagination", he went onto to set up his own animation studio which went bankrupt. It was only later he finally broke through with his character of Micky Mouse. Oprah Winfrey didn't know she would end up as the most successful talk show host of all time. She started out as a TV news presenter and was fired after a few months, having been told by the producer that she was "unfit for television"!

I hope you can take these stories into yourself and drink in good inspiration for staying flexible in your approach to things. All these people had their twists and turns in life, just as we all do. The key thing is not to personalise obstacles; don't make it about you and let that hold you back. I say, get back to higher ground when needed and look from that perspective to re-chart your way. Try different things and be willing to adapt but stay true to your purpose and values.

"Do what you can, with what
you have, where you are"

Theodore Roosevelt

Make Life a 'Get To'

"Attitude is everything, so pick a good one"

Wayne Dyer

On the first page of this book, I started to describe how your life really happens in your brain. The quality of your experience of life really comes down to the quality of your own interpretations of it. It's what YOU ARE TELLING YOURSELF about yourself and your life that makes you feel something. Remember about meanings. If you start feeling negative about something you can bet your brain has created a negative meaning behind it.

Is it wrong then to feel negative emotions? Of course not. Humans are supposed to experience a wide range of emotions, which is why we can. Life, at times, can be darn hard. It may sound negative to admit this, but I think it's more positive to realise this up front and therefore realise the importance of garnering a positive attitude. In a way, can you really afford to live with anything else? If life is going to test you, and it will, better that you ready yourself with some decent emotional muscle.

A Heaven of Hell or a Hell of Heaven

You could be in one of the most stunning places of beauty in all the world yet, if you have a bad mindset, you could nevertheless fail to enjoy almost all of what's around you. We all know of the bratty spoilt child who doesn't appreciate anything and we can train our brain to focus on pernickety, trivial things. Your brain is ready for you to train it to respond in any number of ways; the choice is yours. It gets good at what you get it to do. Just like with anything in life; YOU GET GOOD AT WHAT YOU PRACTICE and this includes your attitudes. Practicing a bad attitude automates it.

Are you going to be one of those people who arrive at a magnificent view only to moan about the climb? Are you going to be one of those people who arrive at a Wonder of The World only to blow a fit at how your sandwiches have got warm? Are you going to be the person who gets the biggest birthday cake only to complain that you prefer Belgian chocolate?! Realise, even if it can feel somewhat empowering in the moment to vent and complain, it doesn't do you any favours.

Fortunately, your brain is flexible and can be tuned up in any way you want, so long as you are committed to doing so. Like I've said, you get good at what you practice. And so, if you want to feel good more often, then practice feeling good. If you want to get good at seeing the best in people and things so that you can have a richer experience of life, then again practice is what's needed. People who take the time to give thanks and feel gratitude train their brains to filter into their awareness more of that to be grateful for. It really is a training process. A person might have a routine each morning where they start their day by writing down three things that they can feel grateful for that day. Once in a while it's good to write out a longer gratitude list of things you are grateful for. As you do so, you force the recognition systems in your brain to adjust.

Remember, what you focus on EXPANDS in your reality and you get good at what you PRACTICE. By participating in practices of gratitude for your life, you enable yourself to feel progressively good. You release the focuses on the negatives and indulge in a far more freeing and happy process. It IS perfectly simple and it's up to you to do so. Start looking at things as a 'get to'; a thing you 'get to' experience in your life, rather than 'have to'. As John Milton famously said in his epic book Paradise Lost:

"The mind can make a Heaven of Hell or a Hell of Heaven"

Creating Your Own Weather System

Creating a positive attitude around things is like creating your own pleasant weather system. You get to enjoy feeling like you are 'in the sun'. If you have a bad attitude, you get to feel like you're dragging a dark rain cloud with you. The thing is, you can continue to feed into your weather system and influence it. If you have a large number of negative thoughts related to someone or something, this is like setting up a new dark cloud and you will have rainy weather to step into when you see that person or do that thing. If you invest in creating positive thoughts about something, when you engage with that thing, you will experience that sunny weather system. In other words, you will be automatically triggered into feeling the positive attachments you've been working on. This isn't necessarily a permanent thing though. Imagine your thoughts and feelings floating upwards towards the sky and adjusting your weather system above you. Put enough new thoughts and feelings through your mind and body and you will change your weather system.

'Get To' Thinking

You are self-programmable and the way you tend to think and feel is due to the self-programming that you've been doing up till now. I don't mean you're a robot, but you are what's called a 'Cybernetic

Organism'. This means an organism which continually gathers intelligence and sends a cycle of feedback from your brain to your body, your body to your brain. You're continually drawing in information through your senses and interpreting it. It's these interpretations that give you room to change your habitual responses and feelings. If you tell yourself better things about what you're experiencing, then you soon get used to thinking that way. The impulses sent from your brain to your body become more positive and evoke a bodily state of positive energy. You will start to think and feel progressively better.

Have you heard of the story of the two Cathedral builders? Two men working in the same job building a cathedral. When asked what job he did, the first man replied, "I'm a Brickie aren't I, I lay bricks. It's hard but it pays the bills. I'm never going even see the end of this building in my lifetime, but I can see the light at the end of the tunnel." When asked what job he did the second builder replied: "Well I am part of an honoured line of workers you see. I build monuments of magnificence to celebrate the Glory of God. One day my son will get to complete the work on this beauty and even one thousand years from now it will still stand tall in all its glory." See if you can be the 'Get To' person. The person who is able to think of things, as things you 'get to' do in life, not have to do.

'Get To's' are created in your own thinking. At first it may take some true conscious effort, but with awareness and practice you 'get to' get better. Have a look at some examples below:

Old Thinking:	'Get To' Thinking:
"I have to cook"	"I 'get to' cook and eat this delicious food!"
"I have to go to work"	"I 'get to' to use my skills and make money so I can tap into the endless ocean of value of other people!"
"I have to clean"	"It feels good to clean. I 'get to' feel that clean, fresh, satisfied feeling!"
"I have to exercise"	"I 'get to' exercise and look and feel at my best!"

Make That Change

My favourite song when I was a boy was 'Man in The Mirror' by Michael Jackson. I always found those words poignant and relevant.

"If you want to make the world a better place

...take a look at yourself and then make the change"

Mahatma Gandhi said, "Be the change that you wish to see in the world".

How can you take these ideas and thoughts now and start to be the change that you want? How can you start seeing your life as more of a 'get to'? Remember, work on your self-talk; you are responding to YOU. Talk to yourself as if you are a victim of life and you will feel that way. Change what you are saying to yourself, and you will change everything: your thoughts, your feelings and your physical outcomes. Take on a 'whistle while you work' approach. Go further and connect your values and life purpose to your work and let it be a glorious mission like the second Cathedral builder.

No matter who we are; what our present life situation is, how old or young or where we're from, we all have two things every day: Time and Opportunity. No-one has more hours in a day than you do, and this gives you all the time there is, to make whatever changes work best for you. In this time right now, be sure to do one key thing for yourself; accept the fact that IT REALLY IS UP TO YOU. You are responsible for making your life as you want it to be. And so, if you want to make your world a better place, then take a look at yourself, recognise all that you've got, that magnificent piece of equipment in your head and channel it to become a force for good.

"Our attitude towards life determines life's attitude towards us"

John Mitchell

Conclusion

I truly hope that this book has had value for you. If so then, happily, I am achieving my purpose. One more hope I have is that you will pick this book up again, perhaps many times. Refer back to its pages and re-do the exercises to gain still further clarity for yourself.

Your purpose is like your North Star, it's always there for you. Your passions and pursuits might not always work out and might change, but your purpose is still there burning bright. When needed, change your approach and realign once again to serve your purpose, even if from round another bend. Write and re-write your values and your purpose to allow them to evolve in your mind. Once written, keep a copy near-by. Make your life a 'get to' by the very thoughts and attitudes you choose to condition in yourself and go and make your life great.

For my part, I wish you joy, success and fulfilment. May you live well, make the world a better place, enjoy life fully and help others do the same.

Spread Your Wings

Spread your wings
It's time to fly
You're here for a reason
Don't be shy

Spread your wings
And aim for the sky
Embrace your life
Always say "Hi"

Breath deep, trust life
Don't fall for a lie
Spread your wings
So we all get to fly

About the Author

James Brannan is a professional Hypnotherapist and Psychologist based in England, with training in Psychology, Life Coaching, NLP and other related change techniques. He offers one on one sessions to those who can benefit. If you are interested in working with James or hiring him to speak at your event, you can make contact through his website www.jamesbrannan.co.uk

Printed in Great Britain
by Amazon